Praise for *Auth*
Exploring the Mysteries o

LaMar Boschman's leadership in worship is a continuing gift of the grace of God to the Church today. His timeless promptings to our pursuit of God's praise and glory are worthy of our attention.

—JACK HAYFORD

Throughout the Bible, we read about people worshipping God. But what exactly does this mean? And what should it look like for us in the Body of Christ? In his new book, *Authentic: Exploring the Mysteries of Real Worship*, my good friend, LaMar Boschman, reveals what it means to truly worship God and shares how we can experience a deeper and more intimate relationship with Him.

—ROBERT MORRIS
Founding Senior Pastor
Gateway Church, Southlake, Texas
Best-selling author of *The Blessed Life,*
The God I Never Knew, Truly Free, and *Frequency*

LaMar Boschman is one of the greatest authorities and teachers on the subject of worship today. His Master's gift makes his writings and lectures bless thousands and thousands of people in the United States and around the world. It is with great joy that I recommend this book.

—ANA PAULA VALADÃO
Multi award-winning and
multi-platinum worship leader

I run into people all the time all over the world whose lives have been changed through their exposure to LaMar and his ministry. I feel the blessing from his legacy on a daily basis. You're about to receive insights from a pioneer in today's worship movement. Get ready to go deep in truth and high in the glories of Christ.

—BOB SORGE
Author of *Exploring Worship*
BobSorge.com

AUTHENTIC

EXPLORING THE MYSTERIES OF REAL WORSHIP

AUTHENTIC

EXPLORING THE MYSTERIES OF REAL WORSHIP

WITH STUDY GUIDE

LAMAR BOSCHMAN

Authentic: Exploring the Mysteries of Real Worship
Copyright © 2017 by LaMar Boschman
Revised and expanded edition. *Exploring the Mysteries of Worship: Twelve Weeks of Worship, A Practical Study Guide* was originally published by Worshipinstitute.com Publishing in 2005.
LamarBoschman.com

ISBN: 978-1-945529-35-1 paperback
ISBN: 978-1-945529-36-8 eBook
First Edition printed 2017
Library of Congress Control Number: 2016952396

We hope you hear from the Holy Spirit and receive God's richest blessings from this book by Gateway Press. We want to provide the highest quality resources that take the messages, music, and media from Gateway Church to the world. For more information on other resources from Gateway Publishing, go to gatewaypublishing.com.

Gateway Press, an imprint of Gateway Publishing
700 Blessed Way
Southlake, Texas 76092
gatewaypublishing.com

This book is dedicated to the explorers and pioneers of worship worldwide who heard a word in the presence of God and mined out the revelation from His Word. They described and declared things about worship that did not exist, but then came to pass. They pointed the way to greater heights in the worship of the Almighty. These women and men gave us tools and principles to lead God's flock to the green pastures and still waters of His manifest presence.

These unsung heroes blazed trails for today's worshippers. The worship artists of today owe them a great debt. For without the revelation they shared, those who followed would have no platform. Today we worship in freedom and with abandon because of their gifts and God's grace upon them. This book honors the fathers and mothers of the worship reformation that brought us these glorious days of praise and worship.

The pursuit of truth and beauty is a sphere of activity in which we are permitted to remain children all our lives.

—Albert Einstein

Contents

Foreword
by Mark Harris

Worship is the way we show our love to God and experience the goodness of His presence. Over the years, worship has been expressed in a number of ways. Regardless of the *how*, the *why* remains the same—*to connect with God*. If you have ever experienced the manifest presence of God, nothing else compares.

God created us with the desire to worship; it is in our bones. All creation, including and especially human beings, eventually worship. Jesus said that if humans would not lift up their voices in worship and praise, the very rocks would cry out in our place (Luke 19:40). Because of this truth, we must know what it means to worship so that we can take our place in history as worshippers of the One True God.

Over the last 40-50 years, a revival of worship has taken place in the church. Much of this revival has happened through music. Contemporary worship music has helped millions of believers connect to the presence of God. Since worship is such a huge part of who we are and what we are created to do, we need a better understanding of God's plan for it.

For more than two thousand years, believers have discussed and debated the *who, what, why* and *how* of worship. For the last 40-plus years, LaMar Boschman has been helping the church understand this very topic. Through writing and teaching about worship, he has devoted his life to helping people connect with God. As a noted speaker, LaMar has influenced pastors, worship leaders, and worship team members, and as an author, his books have been read by students of worship around the world.

LaMar made a profound impact on me as a college student. One of the first books I read while studying at Lee University was *The Rebirth of Music*. For the last several years, I have had the privilege of getting to know LaMar and his wife, Kimberly. I have also been blessed by his teaching on worship.

In this new book, *Authentic: Exploring the Mysteries of Real Worship*, LaMar once again dives into the subject. If you have ever wanted to explore what God thinks about worship, wondered if He hears our worship, and wanted to know what happens in the heavens when we worship, this book is for you too. Maybe you just need to be reminded of who God is and why He is worthy of worship. If so, this book is for you. The mysteries of God's majesty and greatness are thoroughly unpacked in this book.

I hope *Authentic* inspires you as much as it did me. I am grateful for LaMar and the insight and wisdom God has given him on this subject.

Preface

This book explores the truth of worship and what is true about the veneration of the God of all creation. Much is not true about worship. For example, worship cannot be reduced to a program, a set of songs, or a genre of music. If you search the internet for sound teaching and rich revelation about worship, you will likely find endless links about how to play songs on specific musical instruments.

My guess is that most people think they know all they need to know about worship. But all that is changing. An increasing number of young leaders are searching for authenticity in both worship and life. They ask questions like "What is genuine worship?" and "How can I please God in my worship?"

So jump into the deep end of the pool with me and explore the vastness of the realities of genuine worship. Together we will find the diamonds and pearls, those priceless things about adoration, which overwhelm the angels and cherubs who stand before the throne of our Omnipotent Potentate. Only a *created being* can appreciate standing before the face of the *Creating Being.* So we stand in awe in the presence of the Wondrous Mystery, the One who is unexplained and uncontained, incomprehensible, and indescribable. We are overwhelmed with the gravity and profundity of His Holiness as we ascend and transcend in worship.

The exploration of the authentic and transcendent worship of the Eternal King of Glory is to glimpse into the invisible, to know a little of the unknowable, to comprehend a bit of the unfathomable, and to experience the essence of the glorious Eternal. We explore, investigate, and examine the adoration and veneration of the God of Wonder. These great things are beyond the realm of human minds and machines, beyond the noise of the mechanical and the musical methods of mortals. Instead, we feel an inner pull of the Spirit of God and the God-created human spirit intertwined in a delicious dance of deep devotion and mutual affection.

Acknowledgments

I am indebted to the mentors who have impacted me with their discoveries about the essence of true worship:

Jack Hayford, who was part of the beginning of the reformation of worship and was bold enough to preach about worship and reform our thinking on the subject. Sitting under his teaching and reading his books helped form my views in untold ways. *Judson Cornwall,* a profound Bible teacher, was one of the first to put into words the essence of worship. He was also a prolific author, fueling the fire of the worship reformation. His articulate teaching and many books are pylons in the foundation of my views of worship. *Robert Webber* influenced me with his panoramic view of worship across the landscape of Christianity. I saw through his eyes the place that worship has in the diverse communities of God's families of worshippers.

I would like to express my gratitude to my local church:

Founding Senior Pastor Robert Morris started equipping the people of *Gateway Church* and the greater Body of Christ in the truths of worship when few other prominent leaders were teaching about the subject. He and *Lead Executive Senior Pastor Tom Lane* have encouraged me personally when I went through the dark season of not being able to worship because of God's dealings in my heart.

Thank you to Christ For the Nations Institute:

I especially offer my sincere appreciation to *Lawik Joundi*, Academic Dean, and *Jonathan Lewis*, Director of Worship Major. They provided learning and teaching opportunities that helped me forge and fine-tune the concepts in this book.

Thanks are also due to Gateway Publishing:

Thomas Miller, Executive Senior Pastor of Gateway Church and *Craig Dunnagan*, Executive Director of Gateway Publishing, wanted this book to become a reality and a tool to help the local church grow in worship. Gateway Publishing helped develop this manuscript into a published work of excellence. Thank you to the gifted publishing team of *John Andersen*, Director of Book Publishing; *Kathy Krenzien*, Associate Director Operations and Production; *James Reid*, Creative Director; and *Jenny Morgan*, Publishing Specialist in Operations and Finance.

I acknowledge the contribution of the young leaders whom I have mentored, which has been my privilege:

They helped me to forge the truths of worship out of the rock of God's Word. This book is the result of our attempt to put into words how we would explain worship to our worship teams and local church families. Thank you for hours of dialogue and discussion that initiated this published work.

I am ever grateful to my wife:

Kimberly, your unending encouragement gave me the courage to put into words the things that God was showing me. Your selfless love and constant support gave me the boldness to write large and loud. Thank you, my love.

Introduction

Have you ever wondered what God thinks of your worship? When you worship, how do you know if you are really worshipping God? Can you recognize true, spiritual worship when you see it? Can you clearly explain to someone else what true worship is?

During the course of this study, you will make some exciting discoveries that will renew and empower your worship of God. You will understand and be able to communicate to others clearly what true worship is, and you will find a new level of intimacy in God's presence through worship.

Confusion

When most Christians hear the word worship, they automatically associate it with singing a song. The truth of the matter is, worship has little to do with music. Worship is not the act of playing a guitar or singing a song. Worship is not music, art, or even prayer. It is not giving an offering, a weekend service, or following a liturgical form. Though these things can be expressions of worship, they are not of themselves worship.

So the question remains: "What is worship? What is the genuine center and substance of true, spiritual worship?"

Mystery

The worship of God is mysterious and difficult to define. It is inexplicable, unsolved, peculiar, and mystifying.

Worship is not mechanical, systematic, methodical, or formatted. It isn't prearranged, ordered, prepared, controlled, structured, logical, or produced.

Worship is not science, art, or a program. You cannot approach it cerebrally or rationally. Spiritual worship cannot be intellectualized, standardized, or ritualized. We can call our liturgies worship, but alone they can remain routine actions without the essence of true worship.

True worship is spiritual. It is mystical, unseen, ethereal, and supernatural. Real worship is alive and in the moment.

Worship is also relational. It is more about who you love, with whom you are connected, and who you care for. Real worship is more about who you are than what you do. It is about relationship with the great, indefinable, and incomprehensible God of heaven and earth.

Worship is organic, raw, and unprocessed. It has to do with feelings, attitudes, and spiritual things. Spiritual worship is living, animated, and full of emotion.

Discovery

Although worship is somewhat intangible, there are facets of it that can be discovered and experienced. You will find the joy of a deeper unveiling of what worship is and a greater expression in worship.

You will find the study of worship very rewarding and exciting because there is so much to discover about how we mortals adore and interact with an exquisite, magnificent, and immortal One who alone is God—a God who is worshipped by all creation and all creatures in earth, sea, and sky. Worship is the substance of the activity of cherubs and seraphs, angels and elders. It concerns fallen angels and archangels and all things in heaven and earth. True worship most certainly concerns you and me.

Your challenge is to see worship's substance, know its essence, feel its passion, and smell its sweet fragrance. Once you have fully grasped it, owned it, and lived it, then explain it to your children, your neighbor, your life group, your team, or your congregation.

You may find fresh expressions of worship in obeisance, raised hands, bowing, clapping, spontaneous singing, and so much more. Even after a lifetime of studying and writing on worship, I have not found the end to its beauty and depth. Worship is like the love you have for your spouse. The longer you are married, the deeper your love grows as you discover new feelings and expressions of your love.

The Challenge

To craft a simple, concise study of something that's a mystery is certainly not easy. Many Christians have spent their entire lives wrestling with the questions: What does God think of my worship? How should I truly worship God? For that matter, what is true worship, and how do I explain it to someone? I firmly believe that worship is one of the most exciting subjects that a Christian can study.

There are many ways writers and scholars have tried to define worship. Here are a few approaches others have made:

1. We can begin by examining the first time worship is mentioned in the Bible.
2. We can study the derivations of the word *worship*.
3. We can study the Greek and Hebrew words used for worship and then evaluate the frequency with which each word is used.
4. We can read what your heavenly Father and Jesus said about worship.
5. We can look at worship in the tabernacle, the tent, the temple, and synagogues.
6. We can research what the apostles said about worship.
7. We can look at what the Church fathers and reformers said about worship.
8. We can investigate how the early Church worshipped.

9. We can discover how worship evolved throughout biblical and Church history.

10. We can even catch a glimpse of worship in heaven.

These would all be significant and rewarding studies. Some would be helpful in our quest and others are not as relevant to the discovery of authentic, spiritual worship.

Through this study we will explore the who, what, where, when, why, and how of worship. My prayer is that you will have a fresh encounter with the presence of God, your worship will be renewed, and you'll discover the joy of deeper affections and greater expressions in your adoration of God.

—LaMar Boschman

1

Wired

Worship is a universal urge, hardwired by God into the very fiber of our being—and an inbuilt need to connect with God.

—*Rick Warren*

The big black SUV pulled up to the courthouse. Three men in black suits and sunglasses jumped out and surrounded the vehicle. One of them opened the back door.

The crowd that had been there since dawn began to scream.

"There he is!" One woman yelled.

There was the white glove. There was no doubt who this celebrity was.

"Michael!" the crowd screamed, trying to get a response from their idol.

The glove waved back as Michael slipped out of the SUV, walked around the vehicle and up the steps of the courthouse with his entourage.

I couldn't believe what I was seeing as I watched this on television. What fanatical fans—so overcome with his persona, and spellbound by Michael Jackson's star status.

Fans had come from all over the world to support him. One woman even quit her job just to stand outside the courthouse every day for months. She was willing to pay whatever it cost to be close to her American idol. Why would she go to such extreme lengths just to get a glimpse of her idol? The answer is simple: she is wired to worship.

God Made Me Do It

When anthropologists study a civilization, one thing they examine is what the people in that culture worshipped. Worship is an integral part of every culture. Every civilization in all the earth, through all of history, has worshipped something or someone.

Everyone worships something. It could be such things as statues, idols, witch doctors, spirits, wealth, power, nobility, institutions, an idea, a fantasy, a god, and even the Lord Jesus Christ. The study of a civilization's worship is a study of what that culture values and esteems.

Romeo worshipped Juliet. Julius Caesar worshipped his throne. An NBA star worships basketball, and his fans worship him. Worship is universal. It is inherent in all humans to worship.

Being a worshipper is a condition that God put in man. God created you to be a worshipper. You don't need to be trained in worship or have a worship degree. It comes naturally, and it's a part of who you are.

The apostle Paul said,

> And He has made from one blood every
> nation of men to dwell on all the face of the

earth, and has determined their pre-appointed times and the boundaries of their dwellings, so that they should seek the Lord, in the hope that they might grope for Him and find Him, though He is not far from each one of us (Acts 17:26–27).

God has determined where all humans would live so that they would search for Him and find Him. That radar in each person is there so we would search for Him and worship Him. You were created with a desire and proclivity to worship. Every one **YOU WERE WIRED BY THE CREATOR TO BE A WORSHIPPER.** of us is, fundamentally, an unceasing worshipper. That is how your eternal spirit is made. You were wired by the Creator to be a worshipper.

Pastor Jack Hayford said it well: "Worship deals with whom I seek, and the seeking has to do with what I pursue and to what I submit."[1] God has made all of us to seek Him, and that is the driving force in worship.

Everyone Does It

Harold Best said that worship "includes the entire human race. Worship is not just about Christians, but about all people everywhere who are going about their worship, their submission to whatever masters them, and their witness as to why they live the way they do."[2]

WHATEVER YOU VALUE THE MOST IS WHAT YOU WILL ESTEEM, ELEVATE, INVEST IN, AND ADORE.

Worship is about value because people automatically gravitate toward the things they value. We have a drive to seek what we value. Whatever you value the most is what you will esteem, elevate, invest in, and adore. Worship is our expression of what is of most worth to us. It could be a job, a status, a sport, a feeling, a person, or an activity. What we adore automatically becomes a behavior or pattern of life.

That Thing You Do

A corporate executive who places a high value on his accomplishments at work will passionately give himself to achieving status or influence in his job. He may leave for the office at 4 a.m. to beat the traffic and get some work done before the day begins. He stays late and misses the dinner his wife has prepared. By the time he gets home, his children are already in bed. This occurs repeatedly; as a result, his children grow up without spending much time with, or really knowing, their father.

There are times when one must work hard, start early, and perhaps stay late. When a company or project is in crisis, or one needs to meet a necessary deadline, it's important to put forth the extra time and effort. However, when a person repeats this behavior day after day and year after year, he is demonstrating what he values, and therefore, worships. He has an appetite for achievement and accomplishment. He is demonstrating that he values his work over his loved ones. It could be said that he worships his achievements at work.

I had a friend who had an insatiable craving to make money. As a stockbroker, Josh had the perfect job to do that. When the stock market did well, he sold feverishly, pushed the hot stock, and made the big deals.

As a Christian, Josh felt bad about the times when he convinced buyers to purchase stock that he knew would not be a good investment. Yet, he did it because he wanted the cash. The man was driven to make money. I later found out that he was addicted to heroin. He craved the feeling the drug gave him. He lived for it, valued it, and thought about it day and night. You could say that he worshipped heroin and would do almost anything to get some.

I was disappointed in Josh. He spent countless hours violating his conscience, obsessing about making quick money, disobeying the Holy Spirit's convictions, engaging in illegal activity, and harming his body. He lived for the power and the rush; his drive to worship was focused on the wrong thing, and it destroyed his life. Ultimately he ended up in prison and lost his family. He worshipped money and drugs.

These are extreme examples. But through them, you can recognize if there are possessions, passions, and pursuits in your life that you may be driven to worship.

The Path

So, how can you know what you really value, and ultimately, worship? Look at the things that you do. Your actions

THE TRAIL OF YOUR AFFECTIONS AND ACTIVITIES WILL LEAD YOU TO THE THRONE OF WHAT YOU WORSHIP.

speak loudly about what you value. Trace the path of your time, energy, money, and activity. The trail of your affections and activities will lead you to the throne of what you worship.

You don't have to act illegally or immorally to be driven to worship something. What you worship could be as subtle or seemingly harmless as shopping, fishing, sports, or even a fixation on yourself.

The truth is that worship fuels your actions. Who or what you worship shapes your behavior. Therefore, your behavior reveals the object of your worship.

We Are Good at It

When you value something, you aren't stingy about worshipping it. You don't ration your worship. It gushes out. You give all your passion in pursuit or esteem of it. You give lavishly and generously to the object of your affections. You will buy the clothes, spend the time, and drive the miles to do or see what you worship.

Worship flows seamlessly and shamelessly out of who you are. You may not realize it, but you are really good at worshipping! You don't have to work at it too much—it just happens.

Worship Happens

Worship is abundant and everywhere. People adore and esteem things freely and generously. From sports arenas to concert halls, from coffee bistros to rave clubs, people worship all day long. Just as life happens, worship happens.

Worship occurs in extreme sports, colonial reenactments, paintball, the WWE, NASCAR, college football, religion, and soap operas. Body builders, supermodels, rock stars, TV anchors, CEOs, mafia bosses, terrorists, peace activists, scientists, back-to-nature hippies, and politicians all worship. Worship is constantly occurring everywhere by everyone around the world.

I know a guitar player on a worship team who loved how he looked. He would walk up on the platform when it was time to play his guitar and glance down at himself. At picnics, he would wear sleeveless shirts to show off his muscles. Any time he passed a reflective surface he would check his face and hair. He took himself too seriously!

Were his actions normal behavior? They probably were not. One could say he adored himself. However, to some degree, we all do something like that. There might be something that we are excessive or extravagant about. When we are excessive in our behavior, we are probably worshipping.

You Decide

Whatever you do, do with a passion for the Lord:

> Not to us,
>> O Lord not to us but to your name be the glory (Psalm 115:1 NIV).
>
>> Work hard and cheerfully at whatever you do, as though you were working for the Lord rather than for people (Colossians 3:23 NLT).

These Scriptures tell us that whatever endeavor we pursue, it should be with all our hearts as if to the Lord. Your affection in that activity should be directed to Jesus. Then what you do in that activity is worship.

The Lord Jesus, who sits on your heart's throne, is whom you should esteem. No other person or thing should come before Him. Direct your affections to Jesus, the Savior and Lord of your life. In essence, everything you do should be as if you are doing it to the Lord. That attitude of honoring and adoring Him in everything you do is what He considers worship. Attitude and actions comprise worship, and are related. Like love, worship is both something that we feel and something that we do.

Alliances and Allegiances

So I ask you, what do you value? What do you align yourself with? To what or whom do you give your time, energy, or money? What consumes and controls you?

Are you able to see the paths that lead to possible thrones in your life? That might help you see the things that you esteem or worship the most. Are you bowing your heart to someone or something other than Jesus? Will you make Jesus the supreme object of your affection and adoration?

Study Guide

1. What have you seen people worship?
2. Why do people worship these things?
3. What do you value?
4. Have you worshipped (valued or adored) someone or something above God?
5. To whom or what do you give your time, energy, and money?
6. How can you give God your exclusive worship?

Scripture and Reflection

Read Psalm 115 and Psalm 135

1. In what areas have you given too much of your time and resources?
2. What are the paths that lead to possible thrones in your life? What, or who, sits on those thrones?
3. Knowing that we all worship something or someone, which of your activities and attitudes will you adjust toward the things you value?
4. How will you make Jesus the only object of your worship?
5. In your own words, summarize the theme of this chapter and how it applies to you.

Prayer

Heavenly Father, You are the most important Person in my life. You created me and redeemed me, and for that I am eternally grateful. I now realize that I've worshipped other things besides You. Please forgive me. I reaffirm that You are the Lord of my life and the only One that I adore. I trust your Holy Spirit to teach me and equip me to be a better worshipper of You. In Jesus' name, Amen.

2

Morphed

We become what we worship.

—*G. K. Beale*

W hen he entered the coliseum, his jaw dropped.
Wow! What a crowd, he thought to himself. *This is a movement and I'm part of it!*

They had all come to see their favorite rock star.

The band rocked and the fans screamed. Most of them were wearing the band's T-shirts. They even had their rock idols' haircuts and body piercings.

The music pounded. He could feel the bass on his legs a hundred feet away. Such power! The place was electric.

"We love you!" a fan nearby yelled out.

"We want to be like you!" another shouted.

He looked around and realized that almost everyone had a similar look to the rock star. What faithful followers!

The star growled out his lyrics: "I am the man. Hate is my plan. Let's kill everyone we can. God can sit and watch."

The crowd screamed, "Kill everyone!"

They raised their fists in the air and anger filled their faces. Fights broke out to the left. Security was scrambling to control the riot that the rock star created. They all wanted to hate, just like he sang. The fans took on the anthem and nature of their rock idol.

Transformation

Worship is a shaping influence. Worship shapes, or *morphs* you. Whether for good or for bad, you will become like what you worship.

> The idols of the nations *are* silver and gold,
> The work of men's hands.
>
> Those who make them are like them;
> *So is* everyone who trusts in them
> (Psalm 135:15, 18).

Another Scripture says it like this:

> The idols [of the nations] are silver and gold,
> The work of man's hands.
>
> Those who make them will become like them,
> Everyone who trusts in *(or worships)* them
> (Psalm 115:4, 8 AMP emphasis added).

Entire cultures of music, fashion, and lifestyle grow out of what people worship. Rapper fans dress, talk, and act like their icons. Star Trek fans become Trekkies. Extreme Elvis fans become Elvis impersonators.

THERE ARE NUMEROUS WAYS THAT PEOPLE TRANSFORM INTO WHAT THEY WORSHIP.

There are numerous ways that people transform into what they worship. The objects of their worship shape their lifestyle, environment, appearance, thoughts, and actions. Many times, violent sports create risk-takers. Pornography sometimes creates adulterers and rapists. Misguided religion can create extremists. The love for money can create risk-takers. Addictions can create whores and thieves, and an obsession for power often creates abusers and tyrants.

This kind of misdirected worship will never bring you peace or fulfillment, because you are wired to worship Jesus and no one else.

> But we all, with unveiled face, beholding as in a mirror the glory of the Lord, are being transformed into the same image from glory to glory, just as by the Spirit of the Lord (2 Corinthians 3:18).

When you worship the Lord regularly and consistently, you are changed to be more like Him. When you worship Christ, you become Christ-like. This Scripture says that beholding Him and spending time in His manifest presence progressively morphs you into His image.

Who Are You?

All mankind worships, and all of us are being shaped by what we worship. You may not know it, but you are becoming like the person or thing you adore. What you worship determines the direction of your life.

The rock star, supermodel, politician, body builder, and sports star are all influenced and directed by what they value. The worship of people, money, power, notoriety, stature, and achievement, changes the worshipper. You might compromise your character and make excuses for your behavior because of your passion for something.

If your passion for something is intense and out of balance, you can become like it, taking on its nature. You might then become self-centered, vain, indulgent, proud, and narcissistic.

Jack Hayford, in his book *Explaining Worship* says, "The gods that are worshipped begin to manifest their attributes in the worshipper. So in worship you are making the decisions about what your values are, what your priorities are, and what you're going to become."[1]

If you worship money, you become greedy. If you worship sex, you become lustful. If you worship power, you become forceful. If you worship God, you take on the nature of your heavenly Father; you become Christ-like, and you naturally bear the fruit of the Holy Spirit.

Worship is connected to your character. It naturally flows out of who you are and what you value. Your attitudes and

YOU WORSHIP WHAT YOU GIVE WORTH TO.

actions come out of who you are as a person. You worship what you give worth to.

Your worship of God in public services cannot just be turned on and off on weekends. If you value and esteem God, then your worship of Him should flow through your life as it would for anything else. What you do on weekends does not determine if you are a worshipper. It is what you adore consistently, day in and day out, that shows what you worship.

Study Guide

1. What things have you seen people worship?
2. Describe what you saw.
3. How were the worshippers like what they worshipped?
4. Do you believe that people can become like what they worship?
5. Explain how you can take on the nature of what you worship.
6. Describe how you can become like God when you worship Him.

Scripture and Reflection

Read 2 Corinthians 3

1. In what areas of your life have you become like something you might have worshipped?
2. What is the Holy Spirit saying to you about how you are changing?
3. Knowing that we become like what we worship, what will you change in your life?
4. In your own words summarize the theme of this chapter and how it applies to you.

Prayer

Heavenly Father, I acknowledge your supremacy and majesty. I want to become more like You. There have been times when I have esteemed other things above You, and in some ways I have become like them. Please forgive me. I give You my exclusive worship, and You are the center of my life. I want to take on Your character and Your nature. I desire to be more Christ-like. In Jesus' name, Amen.

3

First

The revelation of God is the fuel
for the fire of our worship.
—*Matt Redman*

The essence of idolatry is the entertainment of
thoughts about God that are unworthy of Him.
—*A.W. Tozer*

My heart was pounding in my chest. I didn't want to go in. The counselor was waiting for me. I knew that I had to see him. So I walked up to the front door of his enormous home and rang the doorbell. I had no idea what he was going to say or ask me today.

His office was in the front of his home, so it was very convenient for him to see clients there. He greeted me warmly with a hug and asked me to be seated. He came out from behind his desk after writing something down, grabbed a pad of paper, and sat down on a chair next to me.

We talked for about a half hour. I gave him updates on the struggles I was having, how my job was going, and what I was feeling about life and my relationship with God. Then he asked how my worship life was.

I was embarrassed to tell him that it had become almost nonexistent. I did not have time to worship, with the busyness of the ministry and everything else I was doing—writing books, recording albums, traveling, preaching, and being a husband and father.

"Oh!" he said.

I thought to myself, *What did that mean?*

My counselor carefully shared that the symptoms I displayed suggested I was involved in idolatry.

MY COUNSELOR CAREFULLY SHARED THAT THE SYMPTOMS I DISPLAYED SUGGESTED I WAS INVOLVED IN IDOLATRY.

"Really?" I said. "I love God with all of my heart. I have spent most of my life serving Him and His Church."

"I understand," he said. "Your service and sacrifice is not in question. The question is: does He come first?"

He went on to explain that idolatry is putting anything before God.

"You have put your ministry to God above God!"

"What do you mean?"

"You have valued your service for God—your traveling, preaching, and leading worship—above God and even your family!"

This was news to me! I was completely unaware I had not given God first place in my life.

"By not having time to worship and spend time with Him, you communicate that other things are more important!" He said.

Wow! I was starting to see what he meant!

"When you don't have much time for your wife and your children, it tells me that you value your ministry over them."

"But there are deadlines to finish, my next book, and then we have the big worship event to plan for, and everything gets busy this time of year."

"I understand. However, when that is first and takes priority over your family and your worship of God, it is out of balance and unhealthy for you, your staff, and your family.

"You have made ministry for God more important than God Himself. I'll say it another way. You have made your ministry your god. It is an idol that you bow to instead of God."

My heart sank. I had to fight back the tears. I was shocked!

It had never occurred to me that my actions and attitudes of putting ministry first were so blasphemous to God. I felt horrible. I knew that it would be very difficult to change. I had to be broken of my ambition to grow my ministry.

It sounded vulgar now—*my ministry*. It is not *my* ministry. It is God's! He called me and empowered me with His gifts. It wasn't my talent, charisma, or hard work that would grow the ministry. It was God's grace and favor on it that would bless it. If He didn't bless it, how could I keep it going? What had I done?

I explained to my counselor, "I just want the ministry to meet budget and for it to make ends meet. We have staff to provide for. To provide for them we have to accomplish certain things. There are events to be planned and deadlines to meet." However, the words rang hollow in my spirit.

I didn't want to make the ministry an idol, but I could see that I had. For me, trying to grow the ministry was addictive. I had begun to compare it with other ministries. I had been deceived! My unacknowledged ambition to achieve was a subtle disguise of my drive to be important, significant, and appreciated.

I had made the ministry organization, my status, and the gifts God gave me an idol! I was lifting it up in my heart and mind and bowing down to it. I was even offering sacrifices to this idol—like my family, my time, and my worship of God. I called myself a worshipper and yet I had let my private worship of God slip.

"God, I am so sorry! I repent for making an idol of the ministry and placing it above You," I prayed. "I am sickened that I have hurt my wife and my sons. I never knew I was doing this!"

I had always rationalized working hard for the ministry by thinking it is to help the ministry meet budget and to provide for my family. But, in the deep recesses of my heart, it had taken the place of my wife and children. It had taken the place of God. I was an idolater!

Idols

I am not alone. You might be in the same place I was; putting other things above God. He knows how harmful and destructive idolatry is to mankind. That is why He strongly demanded that we make Him first.

When you worship something that was created instead of worshipping the Creator Himself, you commit the sin of idolatry. This sin is so serious with God that He warned the nation of Israel: if they stopped worshipping Him and worshipped anything else, they would die. He had to get their attention and give them grievous consequences, because He knew how mankind would be tempted to hurt Him and others:

> If you by any means forget the Lord your God,
> and follow other gods, and serve them and worship them, I testify against you this day that
> you shall surely perish (Deuteronomy 8:19).

So serious was the sin of idolatry that God made it the first of the Ten Commandments:

> You shall have no other gods before Me. You
> shall not make for yourself any idol, or any
> likeness (form, manifestation) of what is in
> heaven above or on the earth beneath or in the
> water under the earth [as an object to worship].
> You shall not worship them nor serve them;
> for I, the Lord your God am a jealous (impassioned) God (Exodus 20:3–5 AMP).

In the New Testament, the term *idolatry* began to be used in an expanded manner. Idolatry is not just the actual bowing down before a statue. Idolatry is also applied to placing anything before God, in your heart or affections.

As a worshipper, it is vital to understand the dangerous, deceitful, and vicious nature of idolatry. Although you will probably not make a statue or bow down to it, we do create images in our minds and hearts that we value, and we do bow down to or honor them. I know I did. You must constantly be on guard to let nothing come between you and God.

Idolatry was a grave concern to God because He knows how it hurts and destroys us. He was also protecting us from what idolatry leads to: morphing into something other than what would be best for us.

IDOLATRY IS AN ACT OF TREASON AGAINST THE GOD WHO GAVE US LIFE AND DELIVERANCE FROM SIN.

Idolatry is the human choice of substituting a thing, image, person, or idea for our Creator. Idolatry is an act of treason against the God who gave us life and deliverance from sin. Yet, when we sin by putting other things above God, we declare that God is not good enough, not great enough, not glorious enough, not complete enough, and not all that He claims to be. It says that something else is more worthy to be loved and worshipped.

Idols can be material objects such as houses, cars, or prized possessions. Idols can also be people, whether pop culture icons or your loved ones. Intangible things like fame, reputation, pride, and accomplishments can be objects of worship. Even your ministry or service for God can be an idol. The very gift that He blesses you with, and you give in service to Him, can be an idol and come between you and God.

> Look now, people of Judah; you have as
> many gods as you have towns. You have as
> many altars of shame ... as there are streets in
> Jerusalem. (Jeremiah 11:13 NLT).

Idols can be metal or mental, carved by the hand or the mind. Judson Cornwall, in his book *Things We Adore*, said, "An idol is anything or anyone that is given credit for the abilities that only God possesses."[1] Idolatry mocks God. The worshipper thinks that his idol has more wisdom, more power than God. The idol worshipper says that the idol or star gives him more pleasure than God. He is more satisfied by the idol than by God. In our hearts, we really know that is not true. Christians know better, yet we are prone to turn to something other than God, even though we know that God is All-Powerful, All-Knowing, All-Present.

Our culture does not realize that they have sacrificed so many good things in their lives to the idols they worship. We have so many gods in our capitalistic, consumerist society.

Idolatry comes just as naturally to every human as every other sin. It destroys morality. It devastates lives. It prostitutes our worship. It seduces us and leads us down a path of darkness and deceit with Satan.

Some scholars say there is no more important topic than idolatry. Idols have had so much impact on the human heart; they have ruined many lives. Some have said that at the root of all sin is an idol that has consumed the heart and captured its affections. Idols enable sin to exercise control over our lives and enslave us in chains of bondage. The Bible is full of examples.

Please protect your heart, die to self-indulgence and self-will, and consecrate yourself to God daily as a true worshipper of God.

> Little children, keep yourself from idols
> (1 John 5:21).

All unbelief is idolatry. Any object that I seek or elevate outside of God is, at its core, unbelief—idolatry. To find satisfaction and fulfillment outside of Him is sin. Everything we need has been done and provided in Jesus' finished work. It is a trust issue. Trust that He will provide. Will you rest and let Him do it?

Destroying idols is a personal task. You have to take care of them yourself. Tear them down, break them up, burn them, and bury them, just like Moses burned the pieces of the golden calves. Get them out of sight and out of your life.

Jealous for You

Many people around the world don't know the reality of the wonder of God. They worship their manmade deities, or idols. They are driven to worship something because that is how they are wired. This misdirection of the impulse to worship is so common among humanity that God warned the children of Israel against it:

> For you shall worship no other god; for the
> Lord, Whose name is Jealous, is a jealous
> (impassioned) God (Exodus 34:14 AMP).

God didn't create you to worship simply for the sake of worship itself. Worship has a purpose. You don't sing, clap, rejoice, and pray for your own enjoyment or fulfillment—you do it for the Lord. God is your object of worship—the Holy Father, the Holy Son and the Holy Spirit.

You are not to worship any other thing or person but God. The Lord demands your entire devotion. He shouldn't be fourth, third, or even second, in the objects of your affection. God is a jealous and impassioned God. He is emphatic about being the sole object of your worship.

Jealousy in God's nature is not negative or selfish. The truth is, God is the only true center of eternity, and everything else revolves around Him. He is the Creator of all things, the center of all things, and the reason for all things. Worship should not be directed to any place other than toward Him.

There is nothing more hateful to God than putting another person or thing above Him in priority. It is a shameful libel on His character. It is a monstrous sin to substitute something divinely created in place of the Creator of all things, or worse yet, something you created.

What's He Worth?

Idolatry begins when we lose the sense of awe and wonder of God and relegate Him to a simple concept, which then gets lost in the thousands of other things that bombard our minds daily. To guard against and overcome the ancient compulsion in human nature to create and worship idols, we must see the greatness and supremacy of God. We must see what He is worth! Then the pull that idols have on us begins to fade in comparison.

The old English word for worship is *weorthscipe* or "worth-ship." Through worship you proclaim God's worth. The truth is, worship isn't possible without knowing God and what He is worth. How can a finite human declare the worth of the infinite God when it is impossible for that person to comprehend who God is? How can you, as a creature bound by time and space, know your Creator who is beyond time and space?

Study Guide

1. What does the author call idolatry?
2. What causes idolatry?
3. How did the author commit idolatry?
4. What particular thing in your life did you put before God?
5. How would you define idolatry?
6. Have you seen others give in to idolatry?

Scripture and Reflection

Read Deuteronomy 8 and Jeremiah 11

1. In what ways has it been challenging to put God first?
2. What is God saying to you about idols in your life?
3. How does idolatry affect your worship of God?
4. It is good for God to be jealous of you. Why do you think that is?
5. What will you do to put God first?

Prayer

Heavenly Father, You are All-powerful, All-knowing and All-present. There is no person or thing that is greater and more glorious than you. I repent for putting other things before you. Forgive me of my sins. Expose any idolatry in my heart and cleanse me of it all. Wash me in your blood. In Jesus' name, Amen.

4

Wonder

True worship is based on a right understanding of
God's nature, and it is a right valuing of God's worth.
—John Piper

I stepped up to the podium at Allen AME church in New York City. The musicians had finished singing and playing, yet there remained a lingering sense of God's weighty presence. I knew the message He wanted me to declare. He had put it on my heart earlier, and the moment for it was perfect.

Overwhelmed

I motioned to the keyboardist to keep playing. The open jazz chords were very appropriate for what we were feeling in our hearts. The room was electric with the sense that something unusual was about to happen.

I opened my Bible and read this song:

O worship the Lord in the beauty of holiness;
Tremble before *and* reverently fear Him, all
the earth (Psalm 96:9).

Then I read what Moses sang:

> Who *is* like You, O Lord, among the gods?
> Who *is* like You, glorious in holiness,
> Fearful in praises, doing wonders?
> (Exodus 15:11).

Suddenly, from the back of the church, a woman screamed. Something extraordinary was happening. On the opposite side, another woman started to sob. I had not noticed, but some were standing at the back with hands raised, even though I had begun to preach. I sensed it too. It felt like we were caught up into another dimension.

I continued my message by describing, as best I could, the glorious and illustrious character of God. As I did the pianist went with me—the chords swelled and the bass in his left hand thundered. Surprisingly, a man got up and lay prostrate in the aisle and began to sob. We were in the distinguished presence of the only Holy One. Our hearts were being pulled upward in worship as the glories of the Divine were being declared.

I noticed the tone of my voice had changed as I continued to describe the throne of God and the worshippers in front of it:

SUDDENLY, FROM THE BACK OF THE CHURCH, A WOMAN SCREAMED. SOMETHING EXTRAORDINARY WAS HAPPENING.

Before the brilliantly white throne is a crystalline sea where millions of musicians are standing and endlessly singing spontaneous songs to its inhabitant. The throne is the theme of celestial canticles from every creature in soil, sea, and sky.

It is before this throne that the elders prostrate, creatures fall, and human elders bow. All those before the throne are brought low, kiss the dirt, and humbly bow. It is here we will lay all our prizes, trophies, victories, achievements, rank, and title.

I realized that the power and presence of the Holy Spirit inspired my preaching and the prophetic musical accompaniment. We were getting glimpses of the greatness and the glory of God. We were immersed in a prophetic atmosphere and we were aware of an unusually manifested splendor of God among us.

At times I had to stop speaking because I was overwhelmed. Other times I sang parts of the message. It really wasn't my message any longer. It was as if someone was speaking through me, painting a picture of worship on the other side. I fought back the tears and tried to wipe my nose and not interrupt what was happening. The weight of God's presence was so heavy on us. We were overwhelmed.

I FOUGHT BACK THE TEARS AND TRIED TO WIPE MY NOSE AND NOT INTERRUPT WHAT WAS HAPPENING. THE WEIGHT OF GOD'S PRESENCE WAS SO HEAVY ON US.

Wonder

Three important things happened that night:

First, the atmosphere was well prepared by the worship team, who led us in appropriate songs of praise and worship to God. We sang our way into God's manifest presence.

His revealed essence could be felt among us. The team had chosen the correct songs and led in the way that turned this encounter into a reality.

Second, there were worshippers present who were hungry for God, with hearts focused, receptive, and anticipating meeting God. Our faith was high. We were there to worship and encounter God.

Third, and most importantly, we were contemplating the greatness and grandeur of God, which took us to a higher level of worship. These are key principles in leading or experiencing transcendent worship and the power of God's revealed presence.

To begin to comprehend God, we must look at what God has revealed about Himself, because your worship is tied to a revelation of the divine nature of God.

WHEN YOU REALIZE HIS UNIQUE AND PERFECT ATTRIBUTES YOU ARE INSPIRED TO WORSHIP AT A HIGHER LEVEL.

The character of a person is fundamentally what that person is like; this also applies to God. God reveals to you aspects of His character that inspire your worship. When you study His nature, you will see what He is like. Pondering the character of God invokes worship. When you realize His unique and perfect attributes you are inspired to worship at a higher level.

True worship always flows out of a revelation of God's perfect character. Although to fully understand God is far beyond human comprehension, the Bible does offer several revealing glimpses into His multifaceted nature. As

A. W. Tozer said in his book, *The Knowledge of the Holy*, "The history of mankind ... will positively demonstrate that no religion has ever been greater than its idea of God."[1] What is your idea of God? It is connected to your worship of God.

God Is:

Here are some aspects of God's character to contemplate and communicate and then to transcend in wondrous worship. If you as a songwriter write about these aspects of God, then your songs will facilitate authentic and transcendent worship. If you as a preacher preach about these characteristics of God, then you will see people overwhelmed and undone by His greatness and grandeur. If you as worship leaders and worshippers focus on these attributes of God's personality, then you will be elevated to higher plane of worship.

Self-Existent

God revealed Himself to Moses, saying, "I AM WHO I AM" (Exodus 3:14). God has no origin and exists independent of all other creatures. He is independent in His virtues, decrees, works, and everything else. He is self-existent and self-dependent. He exists for Himself, and man exists for Him.

Self-Sufficient

> And He is before all things, and in Him all
> things consist (Colossians 1:17).

God needs nothing. All that God is and who God is, is in Himself. He contains all and He gives all that is given. All life comes from God and is in God. He upholds all things. He maintains and sustains everything without help from anyone or anything. He has no need for anyone or anything.

Eternal

> Even from everlasting to everlasting, You *are*
> God (Psalm 90:2).

From vanishing point to vanishing point, Yahweh is God. God lives in the everlasting now. He has no past and no future. God dwells in eternity and appears at the beginning and end simultaneously. To God the end and the beginning are the same. He sees them in one view. If we talk about Him in terms of time, we make a serious error.

Infinite

> Oh, the depth of the riches both of the wisdom
> and knowledge of God! How unsearchable are
> His judgments *and* His ways past finding out!
> (Romans 11:33).

When we say God is infinite, we mean that He is limitless, and it is impossible for our *limited* minds to comprehend the *unlimited* One. God is so great that He cannot be adequately perceived. No language, book, painting, or digital imagery can express Him.

Yahweh is beyond definition. God is above all, outside of all, and beyond all that exists. There are no measurements or degrees with Him. God has no intervals, sizes, weights, or distances. He is absolutely boundless, unlimited, indefinable, and uncontainable.

Immutable

> For I *am* the Lord, I do not change
> (Malachi 3:6).

God cannot change in any dimension of His character, purposes, or promises. He does not grow or diminish. God cannot get better or worse. Nothing can be added or taken away from Him because He is forever the same.

He is always consistent in action and character. It is impossible for Him to detour or deteriorate from what He is. There is no mutation of the character of God.

Omniscient

> Who has directed the Spirit of the Lord,
> Or *as* His counselor has taught Him?
> With whom did He take counsel, and *who*
> instructed Him,

> And taught Him in the path of justice?
> Who taught Him knowledge,
> And showed Him the way of understanding?
>> (Isaiah 40:13–14).

The One we worship knows all; He has perfect knowledge of all things. He has never *learned*. He cannot learn something because He already knows everything.

God is the Source and Author of all things and, therefore, He knows all that can be known, instantly and infinitely. He knows every mind, spirit, creature, law, relation, secret, cause, thought, mystery, motion, material, and matter. God knows all life and death, good and evil, space and time; in the past, present, and future.

God is never surprised or amazed and He never wonders about anything. He sees all, so He knows all.

He knows all things about all people, in all places, in all of history, all the time, both excellently and equally.

Wise

> Now to the King eternal, immortal, invisible,
> to God who alone is wise, *be* honor and glory
> forever and ever (1 Timothy 1:17).

HE HAS THE ABILITY TO PLAN PERFECT OUTCOMES AND TO ACHIEVE THEM BY THE MOST PERFECT MEANS.

God is wise and has the ability to judge correctly and to follow the best course of action based on His perfect knowledge. He has the ability to plan perfect outcomes and to achieve them by the most perfect means. He does not guess or engage in conjecture. Everything for Him is in focus and in proper relation to everything else, and He works flawlessly to do what He knows is best.

God acts out of His perfect wisdom for His own glory, for the highest good of the greatest number of people, for the longest time. He works in a way that cannot be improved upon.

Sovereign

> Whatever the Lord pleases He does,
> In heaven and in earth (Psalm 135:6).

God is free to do whatever He pleases at any time and in any place to carry out His infinitely wise purposes with unlimited power. He has sovereign control over the affairs of nature, men, and history.

In His sovereignty God has allowed evil to exist as a renegade fugitive in restricted areas of His creation, in a limited and temporary capacity.

Omnipotent

> And I heard ... the voice of a great multitude ... saying, "Alleluia! For the Lord God Omnipotent reigns!" (Revelation 19:6).

God is all-powerful. Omnipotent means He has infinite power. He is the source of all power and possesses all available power without limit. God can do anything just as easily as anything else. He has so much power that He works effortlessly. He never strains as if He had to muster up more power. He is the Lord God "All-mighty."

Transcendent

> For thus says the High and Lofty One
> Who inhabits eternity, whose name *is* Holy:
> "I dwell in the high and holy *place*"
>   (Isaiah 57:15).

God is exalted so far above and beyond what is human, our minds can never really comprehend Him. He is exalted far beyond our understanding, not in elevation or space, but in quality of being.

God stands apart and above from all that is. He is the highest Being—beyond the reach of human thought. Science can only explore His created laws, and religion can only explore the footprints of where He has been. But the One who walked those paths is transcendent.

SCIENCE CAN ONLY EXPLORE HIS CREATED LAWS, AND RELIGION CAN ONLY EXPLORE THE FOOTPRINTS OF WHERE HE HAS BEEN.

He is the Supreme Being, so He cannot be elevated any higher, for there is no place above Him or beyond Him. Any movement toward Him is elevation for the creature; any movement away from Him is descent.

Omnipresent

> Where can I go from Your Spirit?
> Or where can I flee from Your presence?
> If I ascend into heaven, You *are* there;
> If I make my bed in hell, behold, You *are there.*
> If I take the wings of the morning,
> *And dwell* in the uttermost parts of the sea,
> Even there Your hand shall lead me,
> And Your right hand shall hold me
>> (Psalm 139:7–10).

God is absolutely everywhere. There is no limit to His presence. There is no place that He is not present. God is to our environment as the ocean is to a whale, or the air to a bird. He is even closer to us than our thoughts.

Faithful

The faithfulness of God is a constant theme in the Bible. The psalmist says,

> With my mouth will I make known Your
>> faithfulness to all generations.
> For I have said, "Mercy shall be built up
>> forever;
> Your faithfulness You shall establish in the very
>> heavens." (Psalm 89:1–2).

> And the heavens will praise Your wonders, O Lord;
> Your faithfulness also in the assembly of the
> saints ...
> Your faithfulness also surrounds You
> (Psalm 89:5, 8).

In this same Psalm, God says,

> Nevertheless, My lovingkindness I will not
> utterly take from him,
> Nor allow My faithfulness to fail.
> My covenant I will not break,
> Nor alter the word that has gone out of My lips
> (Psalm 89:33–34).

God's immutability—His unchanging character—ensures His faithfulness. He cannot act out of character and cannot change; therefore, He is endlessly dependable, persistently loyal, and relentlessly reliable. God is perfectly and eternally trustworthy.

> Now I saw heaven opened, and behold, a white
> horse. And He who sat on him *was* called
> Faithful and True (Revelation 19:11).

Good

God told Moses,

> I will make all My goodness pass before you. ... I
> will be gracious to whom I will be gracious, and

> I will have compassion on whom I will have
> compassion (Exodus 33:19).

The quality of God's character that is behind His generosity is His goodness. It is that quality that makes Him kind, cordial, and full of good will. He is tenderhearted, open, friendly, and generous.

God created us and redeemed us because He is good. All of His creatures benefit from His goodness. His goodness sustains and maintains His creation. He has no debt or obligation to His people or His creatures. His goodness is not owed to us and we do not deserve it, yet He gives it freely.

Just

> For the Lord *is* a God of justice;
> Blessed *are* all those who wait for Him
>   (Isaiah 30:18).

The throne of God is filled with righteousness and judgment. He sits not only as King but also as Judge. He rules from His bench with moral equity.

God is compassionate and good; therefore, He is just and right in all His ways. His attributes are never in conflict with one another. When we were born into the world, we were born into sin, and God's justice required a penalty to be paid. But His goodness provided a sacrifice for that penalty, and His Son Jesus paid the debt.

Merciful

> And the Lord passed before him and pro-
> claimed, "The Lord, the Lord God, merciful
> and gracious, longsuffering, and abounding in
> goodness and truth" (Exodus 34:6).

God declared Himself to be merciful as He passed by Moses. Mercy is His nature. We took part in the rebellion to overthrow the King of Creation because of our sin nature. When we were children of disobedience, we made ourselves enemies of God. But because of the merciful nature of God, He has made provision for our guilt and sin to be erased through Jesus.

Mercy is the aspect of God's character that makes Him inexhaustibly and actively compassionate. Mercy is the nature of God that makes Him kind-hearted and empathetic toward you. His merciful nature causes Him to be forgiving.

Gracious

Jonah declared Yahweh's nature when he said,

> You are a gracious God and merciful, slow to
> anger and of great kindness, and [when sin-
> ners turn to You and meet Your conditions]
> You revoke the [sentence of] evil against them
> (Jonah 4:2 AMPCE).

Not only is God merciful but also He is gracious. Grace is the good pleasure of God. It is the aspect of God's character that bestows benefits to the undeserving. He freely grants undeserved favor on us when we are the most unworthy.

Love

John declared in 1 John 4:8, "God is love."

Love wills the good of all and wants no harm or evil. Love desires your eternal welfare. Because God is love, He gives freely to the object of its affection, and God gives generously and sacrificially.

> Greater love has no one than this, than to lay
> down one's life for his friends (John 15:13).

Love takes pleasure in the object of its affection; likewise, God takes pleasure in His children and His creation. He loves all people, of all races, throughout all of history.

Holy

> And one cried to another and said:
> "Holy, holy, holy is the Lord of hosts;
> The whole earth is full of His glory!"
>   (Isaiah 6:3).

The holiness of God is that quality which is His *otherness*. The word holy comes from a root word meaning *separate*. God is *other than* and *separate from* all that is.

Holiness is the crowning attribute of God's character. It sums up all the other qualities about Him. Yahweh is

MORE THAN ANY OTHER ATTRIBUTE, THE HOLINESS OF GOD IS CALLED OUT IN HEAVEN BY ANGELS WHO STAND IN HIS AWE-FILLED PRESENCE.

not only holy, but also holy in the highest possible way. More than any other attribute, the holiness of God is called out in heaven by angels who stand in His awe-filled presence. The seraphs loudly chant in continuous antiphonal melody—singing to one another with zeal and fervency "Holy, Holy, Holy is the Lord Almighty."

Great

> Great *is* the Lord, and greatly to be praised;
> And His greatness *is* unsearchable
> (Psalm 145:3).

Contemplating God's characteristics inspires us to worship. When you see God as the greatest and grandest, the highest and holiest you are drawn to worship Him in a greater way with your greatest praise.

> Praise Him for His mighty acts;
> Praise Him according to His excellent
> greatness! (Psalm 150:2).

How are you to make your praise equal to His excellent greatness? You can't! However, God encourages you to try. Let's make His praise glorious.

Beauty of Holiness

> Give to the Lord the glory *due* His name;
> Bring an offering, and come before Him.
> Oh, worship the Lord in the beauty of holiness!
>   (1 Chronicles 16:29).

We are called to worship the Lord in the beauty of His holiness or otherness, or what makes Him separate and unique. In other words, we are to worship the Lord according to His attributes. Our worship of God should not be focused on the liturgy of worship; rather, it should be focused on Who we worship—His person and character.

This is the mysterious, glorious, illustrious, and wondrous worship of a God. When you contemplate the transcendence of God's nature, the appropriate response is to worship Him. Perhaps you sense that desire to adore Him right now as you read about the character of God, who is unimaginable, incomprehensible and indescribable. Tears have flowed down my cheeks as I wrote of the pristine perfections of our beloved Heavenly Father. When we consider all that He is and done, then our eyes look up, our arms raise, and our spirits soar. At that moment our theology turns to doxology.

Study Guide

1. How would you describe God to someone?
2. What attributes of God impact you the most?
3. Why do those attributes impact you?
4. What particular event in your life was greatly impacted by one of the attributes of God?
5. What is God's crowning attribute, and why?
6. When facing challenges in your life, how will you remind yourself who God is?

Scripture and Reflection

Read Psalm 145 and Psalm 86

1. In what ways has it been challenging for you to know who God is?
2. In what ways has it been challenging to know God's character?
3. How will knowing the character of God affect your worship?
4. In what way will knowing God better affect your day-to-day actions and attitudes?
5. What will you do to know God more?

Prayer

Heavenly Father, You are more majestic and mysterious than I can ever realize. You are high and exalted and greater than I can fathom. You are all-powerful, all-knowing, and everywhere present. You are the only Holy One. Help me understand, comprehend, and experience your mercy, your kindness, and your love. You are magnificent and full of wonder and the sole object of my adoration. As I focus more on who You are, help me by your Holy Spirit to grow in my worship of You. May I make You glorious as I reflect back Your attributes in my life and worship. In Jesus' name, Amen.

5

Called

God has called all of us as priests to minister to God
... regardless of whether we are a congregational
member or a platform musician/vocalist.
—*Robert Morris*

*W*hat is he doing? she said to herself, as her husband
leaped through the yard.

Michal had always been attracted to David ever since the
day she saw him return from war. The women would fill the
streets and sing songs about him. That was when her infatuation for David began. His fame and fortune had increased.
The women would greet him in the streets, singing and
dancing in his honor. David had become a man of power,
strength, and popularity. The entire kingdom cheered and
esteemed Him. He was their champion war hero.

*We are married! Why is he showing off to these young
ladies?* she asked herself.

MICHAL WATCHED FROM THE WINDOW AS DAVID SPUN, LEAPED, AND DANCED BEFORE THE ARK.

*What is his infatuation with
that box? I think he likes that
glow on the Ark of the Covenant
more than me.*

Michal watched from the
window as David spun, leaped,

and danced before the Ark. His expressive movements were not conventional. David was flailing his arms and legs wildly in all directions. He was a maniac, dancing violently with few repeated patterns. He just did whatever came into his mind.

It appeared to Michal that the Ark of the Covenant was the reason for his joyful dancing. The presence of God between the cherubim was the theme of so many of David's songs. He appeared to be so happy now that he could finally bring it home.

Michal couldn't take her eyes off of her husband. His dancing was so unusual. Yet, she didn't like what she saw.

He is jumping around like a gazelle. How ridiculous for the son-in-law of the king to act like this! The longer Michal watched her husband, the more upset she became.

It is so undignified for a member of our royal family to behave like a commoner! Worse than that—a madman! This is the behavior of a worthless imbecile, not a king! With that she slammed the window shutter and walked to the back of the palace.

His lack of dignity and decorum is unacceptable! she fumed to herself. *When he comes home I will give him an earful.* She began to prepare her speech in her head.

When David finally came in the door that evening, she let him have it.

"You made an absolute fool of yourself today ... dancing almost naked in front of the servant girls. You embarrassed my family and me. They are not our people. What were you thinking?"

From that day forward her disdain and contempt for her husband grew. Seeing David worship in abandon had changed their relationship.

Michal was not a worshipper. She despised her husband because he worshipped extravagantly. She would never do that. She wanted to look good in the eyes of the people, as she had learned from her father Saul.

Her stubbornness and disdain for extravagant worship cost her dearly. Never again was she fulfilled or happy. She remained barren the rest of her life. It was embarrassing and shameful to be without child as a Hebrew wife at the time.

Michal did not understand the divine invitation that all humanity has been given to worship God. David heard that call, and had responded from the time he was a preteen. Michal had not. She could not see the necessity to worship and now had grown cold, hard-spirited, and barren.

Created to Worship

All humans are summoned to the throne of God to worship. Worship is the number one responsibility of every believer everywhere. Scripture is clear that it is the universal priority.

> For all nations shall come and worship before
> you (Revelation 15:4).

Your Creator has designed, constructed, and equipped you with the instinctual drive to adore and revere only Him.

Every person, of every generation, of every continent, of every civilization—whether agnostic, pagan, deist, materialist, or atheist— values and worships something.

The Creator has:

> Made from one [common origin, one source, one blood] all nations of men to settle on the face of the earth, having definitely determined [their] allotted periods of time and the fixed boundaries of their habitation (their settlements, lands, and abodes), so that they should seek God, in the hope that they might feel after Him and find Him, although He is not far from each one of us (Acts 17:26–27 AMPCE).

God created you for this time and place to worship Him. He has a desire and plan for you to be a worshipper. That is what *feeling after Him* means.

Instructed to Worship

When a young scribe asked Jesus what is the greatest commandment, He replied,

> The first of all the commandments is: "Hear, O Israel, the Lord our God, the Lord *is* one. And you shall love the Lord your God with all your heart, with all your soul, with all your mind, and with all your strength" (Mark 12:29–30).

Loving and adoring Yahweh is so necessary that Jesus says worship is the chief commandment. Worshipping the Lord is your first and foremost responsibility.

The Bible says that after Jesus fasted forty days, the devil took Him to a mountain and showed Him all the glories of the kingdoms of the world. The devil essentially told Jesus, "I'll give you all of these if you fall down at my feet and worship me. No one is looking; just kiss my feet." Jesus refused to give in to this temptation.

> Then Jesus said to him, Begone, Satan! For
> it has been written, You shall worship the
> Lord your God, and Him alone shall you serve
> (Matthew 4:10 AMPCE).

Here Jesus was quoting the Old Testament commandment to worship God only. He was emphasizing its importance. You are instructed to worship the Lord your God and only Him.

In another instance, Jesus also taught His disciples that they should worship even before they present their requests to God:

> When you pray, say,
>   "Our Father in heaven,
>   Hallowed be Your name" (Luke 11:2).

Hallowed be Your name is a phrase of worship. Jesus is saying that before we start our prayer requests, we are to first worship. The first thing in prayer is to honor God's name (who He is) and put Him above all earthly things. We need to follow Jesus' example by worshipping the name and character of Yahweh before we make our petitions. Before we ask Him for anything, we must first honor Him above all things.

Commanded to Worship

We are commanded to worship. The Holy Scriptures call all of God's creation to worship Him:

> Praise the Lord, O heavens! Praise him from the skies! Praise him, all his angels, all the armies of heaven. Praise him, sun and moon and all you twinkling stars. Praise him, skies above. Praise him, vapors high above the clouds. Let everything He has made give praise to him. ... And praise him down here on earth, you creatures of the ocean depths. ... Let the mountains and hills, the fruit trees and cedars, the wild animals and cattle, the snakes and birds, the kings and all the people with their rulers and their judges, young men and maidens, old men and children—all praise the Lord together (Psalm 148:1–13 TLB).

If angels, stars, planets, the sun, the moon, water, air, snow, plants, and animals are called to worship God, how much more should you and I? Do you think that because nature is praising God, that is why we get inspired to worship when we get close to nature? Perhaps we are subconsciously influenced by the unheard worship of God's creation.

Called to Worship

Throughout the New Testament epistles, we are directed to worship. Peter wrote:

> You are a chosen generation, a royal priesthood, a dedicated nation, and a people claimed by God for His own, that you should show forth the praises of Him who hath called you out of darkness into His marvelous light (1 Peter 2:9 NEB).

A.W. Tozer said God's purpose in sending His Son to die and rise again to sit on His right hand was that "He might restore to us the missing jewel, the jewel of worship: that we might come back and learn to do again that which we were created to do in first place—worship the Lord in the beauty of holiness, to spend our time in awesome wonder and adoration of God, feeling and expressing it. We're here to be worshippers first and workers only second."[1]

Worship should be intrinsic to every believer. Jesus should be the center of your faith and the worship of Him your first priority. Warren Wiersbe said, "Worship is at the center of everything that the church believes, practices, and seeks to accomplish."[2]

Invited to Worship

Oh come, let us worship and bow down;
Let us kneel before the Lord our Maker
(Psalm 95:6).

Mathew Henry said, "He is our Creator, and the author of our being; we must kneel before the Lord our Maker. Idolaters kneel before gods which they themselves made; we kneel before a God who made us and all the world and who is therefore our rightful proprietor; for His we are, and not our own."[3]

The Holy Spirit gently requests your participation in total obeisance to your Creator. He does not demand your worship; He asks for your adoration. Then it is from your own free will that you adore your Heavenly Father. This is how worship leaders and pastors should lead worship: inviting people to worship Him rather than demanding it. Do you hear the whisper of God inviting you to another level of worship?

Redeemed to Worship

Not only were you created to worship, but also you were redeemed to worship. Jesus bought You with His blood for you to worship. Jesus is your Savior and the founder and foundation of your blessed new life. To Him, therefore, you must sing songs of praise and give your worship with eternal gratitude.

You have a worship allegiance to the One who created you and died for you. What a mystery! What good news! You owe Jesus everything. Why wouldn't you spend the rest of your life worshipping Him in endless eulogy and perpetual praise—every moment of every day?

Jesus saved us to be worshippers of our Heavenly Father. As you worship Him, He commissions you to go tell others and invite them to know Him as well. Then they, too, become worshippers. And so it goes.

Benefits and Blessings

Someone asked, "Should you worship God for what He does for you?" No, you worship Him for who He is. When worship is centered on us, it ceases to be worship. Your motive to worship should not be because it benefits you, but because you adore Him. Sincere and heartfelt attitudes toward God, not greediness and selfishness, are what drive true, spiritual worship.

If you worship God to get something from Him, rather than to give something to Him, you make Him your servant and not your Lord. That is not to say there are no benefits to worshipping God. Because of God's goodness, He generously pours out blessings to His subjects. When you leave the King's presence, you often leave with more than you brought.

In Your presence *is* fullness of joy;
At Your right hand *are* pleasures forevermore
(Psalm 16:11).

The presence of God, experienced in true, spiritual worship, will enhance your life and your relationships. The presence of God brings joy to your heart and mind. That joy will spill over into your relationships, making you attractive and pleasant to be around. Living in the presence of God will bring you a happy and blessed life.

A Worship-less Life

There is nothing as sad as a creature that does not want to bless or honor the One who has made him. What a depraved state! Yet some men willfully refuse to worship the Lord Jesus Christ. The rest of creation doesn't have a choice. Even Christians resist worshipping, saying things like: "I don't like this song. The music is too loud. The songs are too wordy; besides, the tempo is too fast."

Worship and its musical expressions are not about you and your musical tastes, but about God and His preferences! If you don't like the words and music, then make up your own lyrics and melodies. Focus on the Lord and look past the style or form to the One who made you and redeemed you.

Priority

There are many reasons why you should worship the Lord. In the end, though, you worship God because of who He is and because of your relationship with Him. You love and value Him above all else because of what He means to you. Worship is your choice, your response, and your priority. Worship is the believer's utmost priority and most noble and highest occupation.

Study Guide

1. In the past, where would worship have ranked on a list of your priorities?
2. What should be your driving reason for worship?
3. Why do you think it is important to worship the Lord?
4. If someone asked you why they should worship the Lord, what would you tell them?
5. How can you motivate others to make worship a priority in their lives?
6. Describe a time when your desire to worship God increased.

Scripture and Reflection

Read Acts 17:22–23 and Psalm 148

1. What areas of your life have decreased your drive and desire to worship God?
2. When is it difficult to be motivated to worship the Lord?
3. Will you do anything differently as a result of seeing the priority of worship?
4. How will your worship be different?

Prayer

Heavenly Father, Forgive me for the times I didn't make worshipping You a priority in my life. I now hear clearly the call to worship You. I want to fulfill the purpose for which you created me: to worship and adore You. You are my Lord, my joy, and my life, and I want to give You my best worship. In Jesus' name, Amen.

6

Devotion

Worship in its truest form is all about relationship.
—*Matt Redman*

She glided past us, her bare feet making feather-light sounds on the floor. Her wrinkled hands were clasped tightly and held close to her heart. I could sense a sweet presence as she passed by. I momentarily lifted my eyes to take a little more in. Her height—or lack thereof—took me by surprise.

This spiritual giant stood not much taller than my six-year-old daughter. She came straight toward two-year-old Jessica and me. Her surprise approach was direct, yet gentle. "Is this the baby who was singing at Mass?" she asked me. "Yes!" I replied.

Donna-Marie continued to describe her encounter with Mother Teresa of Calcutta: "It seemed as if everything moved in slow motion as she, dressed in her simple white sari ... reached out her worn, loving hand to touch my daughter and pat her back. In fact, I think my heart stopped for that moment. That first encounter with this saint penetrated my heart ... remains to this day."[1]

Mother Teresa's profound humility, extraordinary charity, and apparent selflessness touched many lives. She lived

HER LIFE, WORDS, AND ACTIONS WERE ALL WORSHIP TO HER HEAVENLY FATHER.

her life as an act of love to God and mankind. Her life, words, and actions were all worship to her Heavenly Father.

I have a question for you. What would your friends or members of your congregation say if you asked them to describe worship? Would they respond by saying it is praying, singing, reading the Bible, and listening to a sermon? For Mother Teresa it was acts of service.

Mysterious

Some Christians think worship is exclusively singing. Others think that the louder they sing, the more they are worshipping. In some churches, worship is called the order of service. And for still others it is the liturgy. All of these are forms or expressions of worship.

Have you ever wondered why there are so many churches and different forms and liturgies of worship? There are variations in churches because of the differences in doctrine and mission, but there are also differences in definitions and expressions of worship. Since the Bible doesn't reduce worship to a formula, it still remains somewhat mysterious and abstract.

W. E. Vine says, "The worship of God is nowhere defined in Scripture."[2] The lack of a definition of worship in Scripture tells us that God does not want worship to become familiar and formulaic. He does, however, give us clues to understand the mystery of worship.

In English

As mentioned previously, the word *worship* in English comes from an Anglo-Saxon word *weorthscipe,* a noun meaning "someone worthy of honor and reverence." It acknowledges that someone has great worth. The word was later shortened to *worth-ship,* or worship. You would address an esteemed person who should be venerated as "Your Worship."

When we use the word in worship of God, we are declaring His worth. We are acknowledging and agreeing with Him that He is worthy. The twenty-four human elders in heaven declared His worth when they sang:

> You are worthy, O Lord,
> To receive glory and honor and power;
> For You created all things,
> And by Your will they exist and were created
> (Revelation 4:11).

In Hebrew

In the Old Testament the most popular Hebrew word for worship is *shachah* meaning "to bow down, to prostrate oneself before another in order to do him honor and reverence."[3] In those days, if you greeted someone of great honor, you would fall upon your knees and then touch your forehead to the ground as an expression of profound reverence.

> Oh come, let us worship and bow down;
> Let us kneel before the LORD our Maker
> (Psalm 95:6).

In Greek

In contrast, the New Testament word for worship is the Greek word *proskuneo,* means "to kiss the hand with an attitude of reverence." This word also suggested kneeling or prostrating oneself in homage. When someone greeted Jesus with an attitude of worship, they would probably get close enough to kiss His hand or cheek, as was the custom in Middle Eastern cultures.

In contrast, the Old Testament act of worship, to bow, could be done at a distance. The worship described in the New Testament is more affectionate and relational. It had to be done much closer; to kiss the hand or cheek required proximity.

When Jesus died for our sins, He brought relationship to our worship. Yahweh is no longer a distant deity. He has become a Father and Friend to us. You can now draw close because of the blood of Jesus. The change in worship reflects the more intimate relationship we have because of Jesus' sacrifice for our sins.

Attitude

Judson Cornwall, one of the early pioneers of contemporary worship, impacted my understanding of worship. When he was asked, "What is worship?" his reply was, "It is an attitude of heart, a reaching toward God, a pouring out of our total self in thanksgiving, praise, adoration, and love to God."[4]

Worship is your attitude of reverence, love, adoration, or honor toward some object of your affection. That attitude is the very heart and soul of worship.

It is important to understand that before your worship can be an external action it must first be an internal attitude, because your attitudes motivate and affect your actions.

BEFORE YOUR WORSHIP CAN BE AN EXTERNAL ACTION IT MUST FIRST BE AN INTERNAL ATTITUDE

Your attitudes usually express themselves outwardly, giving tangible evidence of the feelings of your heart. In the Bible, God expected His people to sacrifice their best cattle, build altars, give offerings, wave palm branches, sing out loud, and fall prostrate—all expressions of an inner attitude.

Your worship begins with an attitude—then it becomes an action. Your actions in worship without your heart's attitude are empty and without meaning—like sounding brass and clanging cymbals. Your actions can be just noise without affection:

> Though I speak with the tongues of men and of angles, but have not love, I have become sounding brass or a clanging cymbal (1 Corinthians 13:1).

It is important to understand that worship does not start externally; it starts internally. You don't do worship, you mean worship. If you don't mean what you do, then your actions are empty and artificial. That's what happens whenever music, or any action, is rendered to God as worship without meaning. If we call it worship, even though it has the lyrics, the sounds, and the feel of worship, we are deceiving others as well as ourselves. For an action to be true worship, it must have attitude.

YOU DON'T DO WORSHIP, YOU MEAN WORSHIP.

William Barclay said, "True worship is when a person, through their spirit, attains intimacy and friendship with God."[5] It is with our spirit that we connect with God spiritually. To connect your spirit with God, you must be sincere and honestly mean what you are doing.

More Than a Song

The reality is that worship has nothing to do with music or volume. Worship is not the act of playing a guitar or singing a song. It is not giving an offering or following a liturgy.

Darlene Zschech wrote, "Regardless of how magnificent the musical moments are, unless your heart is fully engaged in the worship being expressed ... it is still only music."[6]

God requires more than a song. He wants your heart—your attitudes and motives. Worship does not begin on the platform or with a microphone. It does not start with your voice or your raised hands. Worship has its beginning in your heart. If it is in your heart, then it may be expressed outwardly.

CeCe Winans said it this way: "Music is not worship itself but music is a means of carrying our worship."[7]

Organic

I don't know if you have ever considered that worship is organic. It comes from an organism—you—not an organization or an organized event. Worship does not come from productions or performances. It begins in the heart of every believer, raw and unproduced. Worship comes from God's life forms, His created beings. You are made to express your inner feelings with raw emotion through the organs and organisms that comprise your body.

Sometimes we, as leaders, try to embellish, fine tune, organize, and produce each believer's worship. The trouble is that when man messes with worship, it has a tendency to drift toward form, programs, rituals, legalism, and order of service. Those things have a place to a certain point. But we must remember; worship starts raw and organic. Programs and performances can be like plastic plants, rigid and lifeless. In contrast, spontaneous cries to God in song or prayer are like organic plants—fluid and alive.

If we produce worship too much, it becomes sterile and loses its pure and real essence. It would be like someone producing your date night with the one you love—you are told when and what to say and do. The organic love and affection you have for that person would then become a form and lose the meaning and emotion that was originally in your heart. The person you have affections for may wonder, are you just saying that because you were told to, or do you mean it? They ask because what you are saying and doing does not match your words or actions. They would be suspicious of your true affection if you were doing only what you are told.

True worship is more organic than organized. Real worship has its genesis in *life forms*, not *art forms*. Worship, like any organic life form, morphs and evolves mysteriously. It grows and develops and changes as your relationship with God develops and deepens. Worship certainly is not systematic or mechanical.

Relational

Worship comes out of relationship. In the New Testament, worship is intimate and personal. If you do not have a relationship with God, you cannot worship. You can only really appreciate and adore God when you know Him personally and intimately. Jesus said,

> You worship what you do not know; we know
> what we worship, for salvation is of the Jews
> (John 4:22).

You worship what you know—what you revere and respect. You worship the One you affectionately adore. You worship what you have interest in and feelings for. It is difficult to reverence, appreciate, or adore a stranger; however, it is easy to honor, love, and adore your spouse. The difference is relationship—having intimate knowledge of each other and experiencing life together. Author John Piper once said, "Where feelings for God are dead worship is dead."[8]

Spiritual

Most importantly, worship is intuitive and spiritual. Paul said we are spirit worshippers.

> For we are the circumcision, who worship God
> in the Spirit, rejoice in Christ Jesus, and have
> no confidence in the flesh (Philippians 3:3).

Worship is mysteriously supernatural. It is not of the natural realm. It is more intuitive than intellectual. It is more abstract than concrete and more mystical than physical.

Worship has a spiritual essence and begins unseen and inside. Worship is spiritual because God is Spirit and you are spirit. It is in that dimension that you are to worship. You are to worship *in* and *by* your spirit and God's Spirit. Without the involvement of your spirit and God's Spirit, your worship is not spiritual.

Not Technical

The essence of worship is not mechanical or technical. Technology is the creation of man and bears his fingerprints. Technology can help or hinder real worship; therefore, technology and technique must be submitted to the theology of worship when used in facilitating spiritual worship. That means that spiritual and Biblical principles should determine how to use songs, video projectors, lights, and sound systems in the context of worship.

If these things distract your attention from the object of your worship, they are hindrances. However they can assist the worshipper if they come alongside (not in front of) and tastefully enhance and facilitate the spirit worship of the heart.

Living Worship

Worship is also how you live your life before God.

> Whatever you do in word or deed, do all in the
> name of Jesus the Lord, giving thanks to God
> the Father through Him (Colossians 3:17).

Worship is giving your all in attitude and action for the glory of God. It is doing things with a heart attitude—*This is for God!*—just as mother Teresa demonstrated in her love and care for the less fortunate.

Paul said to those who worked for others that they should be obedient.

> With fear and trembling, in singleness of your
> heart, as unto Christ;
> Not with eyeservice, as men pleasers; but
> as the servants of Christ, doing the will of God
> from the heart;
> With good will doing service, as to the Lord,
> and not to men (Ephesians 6:5–7 KJV).

Do what is right and good for the Lord from your heart and not for attention or self-promotion. You can broaden your capacity to worship as you learn to live as unto Christ.

Study Guide

1. How would you describe true worship?
2. How do you personally know when you are really worshipping God?
3. Have you ever caught yourself going through the motions and not really worshipping God? What did you do about it?
4. How would you describe worship to a new believer?
5. When does an activity become worship?

Scripture and Reflection

Read Colossians 3:12–17 and Psalm 111

1. What are the barriers in your life that keep you from giving 100% of who you are to God?
2. What steps are you going to take to make who you are more God-centered?
3. What activities in your life will you offer to God as worship?
4. What can you change to make your worship more organic, relational, and spiritual?

Prayer

Heavenly Father, today I am reminded that worship is personal, passionate, organic, relational, and spiritual. Help me keep my worship honest and true. I'll give You more than a song or a prayer. I'll give you more than external posture and actions. I will put all my affection and adoration into my worship and keep it real. I want to be true to the devotion of worship. Holy Spirit, help me live a life of true worship. In Jesus' name, Amen.

7

Mobile

Because He never changes, our praise of Him
should never cease.
—*Don McMinn*

The sun was intense as she made her way to the well. It was about noon, and she liked to come when no one else was around. It was too hot for most of the locals. The looks and the questions were easier to avoid that way.

This day was different from the others because there was a man near the well.

That's odd! she thought to herself. *What is a man doing here? It is a woman's job to haul water for the family.*

As she drew closer, He called out to her, "Would you draw me some water? I could use a drink." She didn't know what to say. She should not be speaking to Him.

"You are a Jew! Why are You asking me, a Samaritan, for water?" she asked. "Besides, men don't talk to women here."

He chose this time of day so He could speak to her without the men of the community seeing him. They would probably have beaten Him and thrown Him out of town. They were strict about men speaking to women who were not relatives. That is why He sent those that were traveling with Him to get food. He knew he was taking a risk to talk to this woman.

He didn't respond right away but after a few moments He repeated His question.

"Would you draw Me some water?" Hospitality demanded giving a stranger or visitor a drink of water.

He paused again. Then He said, "If you knew who I was, you would ask Me for the water of life—a free-flowing fountain."

Puzzled by what He meant, she grabbed her bucket and let it down into the well. She pondered His words. *What does He mean —the water of life? He doesn't even have a bucket to get this water.*

She brought Him the water and He drank it slowly, savoring every drop. He knew that Jews considered Samaritan women unclean, and anything they served was considered impure. But He ignored that prejudice and drank the water, enjoying it thoroughly.

The woman said, "Are you better than our ancestor Jacob who built this well? This water gives life to our community."

"This water quenches your thirst for a while, but with the water I give you, you will never thirst!" He knew that she was empty inside and thirsty for more in life.

"Rabbi, give me this water. I don't want to always have to come to this well when I get thirsty."

"First, get your husband, and I then will tell you."

"I'm not married," she replied, embarrassed, lowering her eyes, and looking to the ground. "I don't have a husband."

"I know. In fact, you have been married five times!" He knew that she had failed at many relationships and had a bad reputation in the community.

"On top of that, you are living with a man now and you are not married."

Surprised, she asked, "How do You know this? Are You a prophet?"

Wanting to change the subject, she said, "Well, maybe You can tell me this. Our ancestors worshipped on this mountain," pointing to Mount Gerizim. "Why is it that you Jews insist the only place to worship is in Jerusalem?"

He said to her, "A time is coming when people will worship the Father neither on Mount Gerizim nor in Jerusalem."

She wondered to herself, *What does that mean? If Jews will not go to Jerusalem to worship, and Samaritans will not go to Mount Gerizim to worship, where will we worship? How is that possible?*

At that moment His companions returned with food for lunch. They were surprised He was talking to a woman, and a Samaritan at that. But as good followers of their teacher, they did not question his motives (paraphrased from John 4:1–42).

He Changed Everything

For thousands of years, until the time of Jesus, the public worship of God was confined to a place—Solomon's temple, David's tent, or Moses' tabernacle. During this time in Israel's history, a dispute arose as to whether the place of worship should be Jerusalem or Mount Gerizim. Jesus, however, ended that controversy when He said that neither place would be the place of worship.

The old order of going to a place to worship was passing away. The worship of God was not to be confined to a single place as it had been in the past.

Worship is to occur everywhere and at any time.

WORSHIP IS TO OCCUR EVERYWHERE AND AT ANY TIME.

Jesus teaches us today, as He taught the Samaritan woman, that there is no exclusive place to worship Him. Buildings are dedicated as places for God's people to meet, but they are not the primary places of worship.

> For you are the temple of the living God. As
> God has said:
> "I will dwell in them" (2 Corinthians 6:16).

Samaritans had worshipped on Mount Gerizim for years. They thought, "If it was good enough for our ancestors, it's good enough for us. We must maintain our traditions." When disputes over differences in worship arise, so many people think that they have the high ground because they are following the right traditions and proper order in their worship.

To counter that type of mindset, Jesus strongly insisted in John 4:21–24, "My Father is changing where we worship. The time is coming soon—in fact it is here—when you won't go to Mount Gerizim or to Jerusalem, and those who want to worship Him will no longer offer animal sacrifices, but will worship in spirit and in truth."

Mobile Worship

If someone were to ask you where you worshipped, how would you answer? The vast majority of believers would probably answer the name of their local church. But the truth is that your worship isn't confined to a single location or particular structure. Did you know that you don't go to church, but you are the church? Paul asked,

> Do you not know that you are the temple of
> God and *that* the Spirit of God dwells in you?
> (1 Corinthians 3:16).

It is an Old Covenant and Old Testament paradigm to think that worship only occurs at a building on certain days. Sure, your church building is dedicated and set apart to God for the public worship by God's people. But it is no more sacred than the place where God said He would dwell—you.

YOU ARE A TRANSPORTABLE TEMPLE OF WORSHIP.

Like a mobile home, you are a mobile temple, not with wheels but with legs. You are not limited to one place like immoveable buildings; you are a transportable temple of worship.

Temples are places of worship, so you are also a place of worship. You are a "mobile home" of worship. Where you go, worship goes. Where you go, worship happens. When you go shopping, you can worship. When you go to work, you can worship. When you are at home, you can worship.

I desire therefore that the men pray (*worship*)
everywhere, lifting up holy hands, without
wrath and doubting (1 Timothy 2:8 emphasis
added).

I challenge you to take worship public. Try worshipping
in your car, on the street, and in your home. You don't need
a worship leader or a worship team. You don't need a pastor
to plan the worship for you. You are a priest of God and His
dwelling place. In your own raw, organic, spontaneous way,
worship Him and see what happens.

On Location

Fundamentally, worship is something done in the heart,
not in a building. The focus of the Lord in worship is not a
church sanctuary; it is the sanctuary of the heart.

The Lord wants you to worship every day and everywhere.
Jesus encourages you to worship not just *in Jerusalem or on
this mountain*, but in all places and all spaces. Worship in
your home, on the way to and from work, and in your car.
Make worship part of the rhythm of your life. Take your
worship on location.

Public and Private

You worship better in public when you have first worshipped in private. If you make private worship a habit,

you will not feel awkward worshipping in pubic. Singing, praying, and lifting your voice to God will become second nature to you.

Did you know that you are supposed to sing your worship at home and even in your beds?

> Let the saints be joyful in glory;
> Let them sing aloud on their beds
>   (Psalm 149:5).

Hence, worship is to pervade your private life as well as your public life. You should praise and worship the Lord in your home; in your living room and even in your bedroom.

Timing

The Scriptures clearly teach full time worship. You are to "pray without ceasing" (1 Thessalonians 5:17) and to praise continually. The psalmist David said,

> And my tongue shall speak of Your
>   righteousness
> And of Your praise all the day long.
>   (Psalm 35:28).

The kind of praise in this Scripture is specifically singing praise to God. In this verse David is saying that he will sing to God throughout the day.

There can be no mistake as to how often and how long God wants you to worship:

> Let us constantly and at all times offer up to
> God a sacrifice of praise, which is the fruit of
> lips that thankfully acknowledge *and* confess
> *and* glorify His name (Hebrews 13:15 AMP).

> I will bless the Lord at all times;
> His praise *shall* continually *be* in my mouth
>   (Psalm 34:1).

Worship needs to pervade your public as well as your private life. You are God's temple, and in His temple worship should never cease. Don't act like you are in the military reserves, where you only have to report to duty on weekends. Likewise, don't only worship on weekends. Judson Cornwall, a beloved mentor said, "Worship is always a now activity."[1] God wants you to be a full time worshipper that worships Him all the time and everywhere.

Sabbath Worship

Unfortunately, modern society is driven to work hard; so much so, that we don't know how to worship in God's rhythm anymore. People no longer value *being* over *doing*. In a new high tech world of doers and achievers, the Sabbath appears to be an outdated and foolish tradition.

However, keeping the Sabbath is just as important for a believer as not killing, stealing, or committing adultery. They are all part of the Ten Commandments. These rules are for your good and well-being. Likewise, honoring the Sabbath is good for us. It refreshes and restores the spirit, soul, and body. It is also a day of worship.

You keep the Sabbath because God kept it. He showed us the importance He places on *being* over *doing*. To simply *be* is divine. Our loving, heavenly Father showed how important the Sabbath is to our health and worship life not just because it is one of the Ten Commandments; He said that anyone who violates it should be put to death.

> Work shall be done for six days, but the seventh *is* the Sabbath of rest, holy to the Lord. Whoever does *any* work on the Sabbath day, he shall surely be put to death (Exodus 31:15).

> There is a large, leisurely center to life in which God is to be worshipped. God blessed the seventh day, and sanctified it because on that day He ceased from all the work He had set himself to do (Genesis 2:3 NEB).

On the seventh day, God rested. To *rest* in this context means to cease, desist, neglect, cut off, and interrupt. The Sabbath is a day of rest for the heart—abstinence from labor. The word Sabbath simply means to quit. Stop. Take a break. It is not *just* a day off, however. That is a secularized Sabbath. The Sabbath is not a wasted time. It is a worship time. The Sabbath is a day to interrupt your week, neglect your to-do list, cease your normal activities, and worship—to meditate on who God is, talk to Him, and sing to Him.

THE SABBATH IS NOT A WASTED TIME. IT IS A WORSHIP TIME.

The Pulse of the Day

And there was evening and there was morning, one day (Genesis 1:5 NASB).

The day is the basic unit of God's creative work; evening is the beginning of that day. God created the evening first and then the day. Therefore, you should start your rest in the evening and go through the next day.

God's day begins when you quit your activity and soon go to sleep. The day begins in the evening with Him. You rest and He works through the night. In the evening you quit your work and God goes to work. He makes preparation for you when you arise. The next morning you grab your coffee and step into the day that He has already prepared for you.

Study Guide

1. When is the appropriate time to worship?
2. How often do you worship the Lord during the day?
3. Do you know others who worship often? What is different about their lives?
4. Why is it easy to think of worship as a Sunday-only event?
5. Describe what worship looks like for a full time, lifestyle worshipper.
6. List three separate ways to change your mind-set about where and when you worship.

Scripture and Reflection

Read John 4:1–42 and Psalm 34

1. When in your life has it been difficult to worship?
2. Where is it difficult for you to worship?
3. What will you change to treat your inward man more like God's temple?
4. How will your Sunday, or Sabbath, worship be different?

Prayer

Heavenly Father, You have made me a temple for Your precious Holy Spirit. I desire to please You with where and how I worship. Teach me how to worship You all the time and everywhere. Remind me to worship You at home, at work, and at play. I want Your praises to be on my lips and my worship to bubble out from the depths of my being all the time. May my adoration of You and my thanksgiving to You be the rhythm of my life. In Jesus' name, Amen.

8

Expressions

Worship is love expressed.
—*Robert Morris*

G abe sat at his desk and looked across the second grade classroom at her and smiled. She was so easy on the eyes. Her name was Julie, a perfect name for such a pretty girl. He liked the sound of it because it reminded him of her.

He sat right behind her in class. He could see her curls, so perfectly proportioned on the back of her beautiful blond hair. She was so feminine, and acted very confident for a seven-year-old. She captivated everyone who saw her. At least, that was Gabe's impression.

At recess she would have fun with her friends, and Gabe wanted desperately to join in but did not know how. As boys often do, he thought the best approach was to tease her. So he did. Gabe loved the attention. She giggled. Inspired, he pulled her hair, took her coat, and ran away. With that, however, she was not impressed. Instead of liking him, she was angry. Gabe felt bad.

Now it is the tenth grade, and look at her. She is so beautiful! Gabe's attraction to her had grown, but he still could not tell her how he felt. He enjoyed her company. Since she was his math partner, they would do equations together and get into conversations exploring the solutions. However, those dialogues remained superficial because Gabe's heart was often in his throat when she was around.

One night they were at a youth group party sitting on the porch. It just happened they were alone and he started looking up at the stars. It suddenly dawned on Gabe; now is the time to let her know the feelings he had for her.

He tried to move his hand to touch hers, but it wouldn't budge. It was like it was stuck, or asleep, and unresponsive. Gabe became very nervous and began to perspire.

What would she think of me? he thought to himself.

Okay, I'll tell her. I'll just blurt it out.

Gabe began to speak and the first syllable got stuck in the back of his throat. Some kind of guttural grunt came out. He was embarrassed, and quickly closed his mouth.

She turned to him and said, "Are you all right?"

"Yes. Everything is good." Gabe just couldn't form the words to tell her how he felt about her.

Expressing Feelings

A similar thing happened to me when I tried to express my affections to God. As a conservative evangelical, I had not grown up seeing spontaneous expressions of affection to God in public worship. I envied those who could raise their hands and sing at the top of their voices. For me it was very difficult. Perhaps I was too afraid of what people might think.

Have you ever wished that your worship wouldn't be awkward? Many of us find it difficult to express our worship. You may not worship very well because you don't know what to do to express your feelings to God.

Look at all the ways to praise the Lord in this song. For some of us it is very difficult.

> Praise the Lord!
>
> Praise God in His sanctuary;
> Praise Him in His mighty firmament!
>
> Praise Him for His mighty acts;
> Praise Him according to His excellent
>   greatness!
>
> Praise Him with the sound of the trumpet;
> Praise Him with the lute and harp!
> Praise Him with the timbrel and dance;
> Praise Him with stringed instruments and
>   flutes!
> Praise Him with louds cymbals;
> Praise Him with clashing cymbals!
>
> Let everything that has breath praise the Lord.
>
> Praise the Lord! (Psalm 150:1–6).

Staggering and Stumbling

If you sense an awkwardness or lack confidence when you worship, you are not alone. It is probably more normal than you think. Most people haven't had much equipping or coaching in worship. Perhaps you have not been trained or equipped in how to worship. Like most Christians, you just sort of stumbled into it. Perhaps you started by copying those around you in public worship or doing what the leaders told you.

Your worship might feel clumsy at times as you stumble through a public worship service that someone else has planned for you. Perhaps the worship doesn't fit you and isn't how you would express yourself to God. As a result, you just coast along, watching for your cue from the upfront leaders or the church bulletin.

That kind of staggering through a worship service is not only awkward, but it also keeps your worship from being real and sincere.

Date

Have you wished you had a manual that explained exactly what to do and when to do it? Some people think that worship would not be so awkward if it were codified. Then you could do the right thing at the right time. However, God has not provided a worship manual with step-by-step instructions on how to worship, because worship is more about your spirit, personal attitudes, and affections toward God.

British worship leader Martin Smith once called us "God's Romance." I like this. There is a relational affection that God shows toward us and we should respond to it. God wants your worship to be an expression of your love for Him. Just as when a couple are on a romantic date, they should be themselves and let their feelings for each other determine their actions; not have someone tell them what to do and when. So your love for God at each moment should determine your expression of worship.

The many options of expression you have in worship could make you insecure and uncomfortable if you don't know what to do, especially if the expression is new to you. You might hesitate at times to express yourself because you don't want to be embarrassed.

In the very process of explaining worship, we run a risk of cheapening it. By explaining the ways to love God, we might put more emphasis on the *how-to* and not enough on the love itself. That is what happens in many worship services when the focus is on the song, the prayer, the sermon, or the offering. These are outer actions and not the inner attitude. As we have discovered, the outer actions become worship due to the inner attitude.

The spontaneity of worship is important also because it is a personal expression of what you feel at that moment. You must have the liberty to express your attitudes in a manner true to your heart. It makes your worship honest and personal.

When you are asked do things that aren't you, it is difficult to mean them. When expressions don't come from your heart, they remain empty. Therefore, your expressions of worship should be sincerely affectionate. Worship leaders have a responsibility to help facilitate each believer's

WHEN EXPRESSIONS DON'T COME FROM YOUR HEART, THEY REMAIN EMPTY.

personal worship in a way that enables individual expression and yet remains unified.

Unique Expression

Your adoration and love for God can be expressed in many different ways. The options are almost limitless. Because worship is not formulated, you can find unique and individual expressions that better communicate your heart feelings. You can sing, clap, bow, stomp, dance, jump, lift hands, prostrate yourself, pray, meditate, cry, shout, kneel, give gifts, and so much more. It is for you to determine how you want to bless the Lord. What is in your heart?

Hugs and Kisses

The hugs and kisses that my wife and I share are not the source of our love. It is the opposite. It is the loving relationship we have that inspires our hugs and kisses. In the same way, worship is not driven by the actions of your expressions. It is the loving relationship with God that motivates your actions and expressions of worship.

All too often the visible expressions of worship get all the attention, and people mistakenly think that those actions are worship. They are merely expressions of worship. The real source of worship is the attitude and motive of the heart. That is not to say that expressions are irrelevant. The Bible commands you to sing, pray, clap, shout, bow, and kneel, but all these things must come from your spirit or heart to be meaningful.

Attitude

Just as gas is needed for a car to operate, so the right attitude is needed for worship. If you worship God without the right attitude, you are simply going through mechanical motions. Your expressions are empty and void of meaning.

So, when you have the attitude, visibly express your love and adoration to God. Allow all of these expressions to flow from your heart out of your relationship with God. God created you to be expressive!

God's Expectation

What is your responsibility before God in worship? What does God expect of you in worship? Few bother to ask these questions, and the answer is challenging for all of us.

> So he answered and said, "'You shall love the
> Lord your God with all your heart, with all your
> soul, with all your strength, and with all your
> mind,' and 'your neighbor as yourself.'"
> (Luke 10:27).

God desires wholehearted, full-emotion, full-bodied, and whole-minded worship. He delights in all-encompassing expressions of worship, especially when you mean it.

Think of a toddler coming to their father giddy, happy, clapping their hands, and singing. Do you think the father would enjoy them? Do you think their expressions are coming from their heart? They most certainly would not be faking it or performing. This innocence and honesty in worship is why Jesus said in Matthew 21:16 that praise is perfected in the mouths of toddlers.

Someone once told me, "You can go too far in worship." Is that true? Can you love God and express your love for Him too much? Let me ask it this way, "Can I express my love to my wife too much?" Even though I

CAN YOU LOVE GOD AND EXPRESS YOUR LOVE FOR HIM TOO MUCH?

may think so, my wife would say, "No, not possible!" You cannot say, "I love Jesus with all my heart" and then put a limit on your worship. God expects you to worship Him with all of your capabilities and capacities.

Vocal Expressions

There are many kinds of vocal expressions that you can use to worship your Creator and Savior—shouting, singing, praying, talking, proclaiming, and declaring, to name a few.

Singing to God is emphasized in Scripture in numerous places and has helped define Christian worship for millennia. In fact, Christianity is known as a singing faith more than any other. Singing in worship is an eternal activity, and occurs in heaven infinitely.

Your voice is the speaker of your heart. Singing is an important part of your expression in worship to God because the heart and soul of a person can be best expressed through song. Your vocal tone, color, and emotion are one-of-a-kind vocal expressions of your heart.

Silent Expressions

Another expression is silence, though it may not seem like one. It is a valid expression in worship because, keep in mind, worship is more attitude than action. Silent expression can be through tears, bowing, kneeling, meditation, and sitting quietly. The heart attitude is the important ingredient, and the heart can remain active even in silence. Worship is present, even in silence, if there is attitude. You can have a worshipful attitude and no outward action, and there can still be worship.

As one who has led worship, I would far prefer someone sit in silence and worship over a person who jumps all over the place, and isn't worshiping at all. The inner attitude is what makes worship pure and real.

Motionless Expressions

Being still before the Lord is a very appropriate thing to do when you sense God's nearness. Sometimes you are more receptive to Him when you are motionless. The Scriptures say:

Be still, and know that I *am* God (Psalm 46:10).

It is important to know that you do not have to always do something. You can be quiet in God's presence and worship. You can be motionless and silent, and all the while be passionately communicating with him in prayer and adoration.

Body Talk

Bob Kauflin, in his book *Worship Matters*, says, "Our bodies naturally respond to what affects our souls. I open my arms wide when my daughter runs to meet me. I jump up from the couch with my hands in the air when my team scores the winning touchdown ... I cry when my friend's child dies. No one has to teach us those responses."[1]

God created you to express your worship through body language. The body postures of worship are many, and include standing, sitting, kneeling, dancing, and bowing. You can choose whatever expression matches your affection toward God.

YOUR BODY SHOULD SAY THE SAME THING YOUR VOICE DOES IN WORSHIP.

While you do that, always ensure that your vocal language doesn't contradict your body language. Your body should say the same thing your voice does in worship. When it doesn't, there is a sense that you may not be sincere.

One of the most extreme postures of worship is prostration. Sometimes, when the presence of God is particularly evident, lying flat, face downward on the floor, is the only appropriate posture. I have done this on many occasions when the sense of God's presence was so strong that total obeisance was appropriate.

One of the most popular expressions of worship is clapping. However, people often clap habitually at the end of a song as if they are observing a performance. Clapping should always be done with meaning, attitude, and purpose, and directed to God. The Bible speaks about clapping and shows us it has power and purpose.

O, clap your hands, all you peoples!
Shout to God with the voice of triumph!
(Psalm 47:1).

Clap to God in praise and appreciation for His great works.

Another popular expression is lifting hands. Once again, this active expression needs to be sincere and not habitual. When you lift your hands, check and make sure you are doing it to the Lord and not because it is a habit or something that is expected of you.

> Let us lift our hearts and hands
> To God in heaven (Lamentations 3:41).

The Scripture also says,

> Praise Him with the timbrel and dance
> (Psalm 150:4).

In some circles organized dance movements are an emphasis during worship. Yet they can become routine if they are done by rote or pattern, and not from the heart. If there is no praise in the dance, it isn't worship. It is the devotion in the motion that makes your movement worship. If you have motion with no devotion there is no worship, though you may call it worship dance and be dancing with grace and excellence.

You can have devotion with no motion, and you will have always have worship. Do you see what is most important? Always remember, it is the attitude in the action that makes what you do worship.

Musical Expressions

Another popular expression of worship is music. It come natural to most people, and it is the expression that is most emotional and heavenly. Since the creation of music, its primary purpose has been to worship God.

There are times when God commands us to use musical instruments in worship of the Lord.

> Praise the Lord with the harp;
> Make melody to Him with an instrument of ten
>   strings.
> Sing to Him a new song;
> Play skillfully with a shout of joy
>   (Psalm 33:2–3).

Have you ever noticed that the music in the Bible is often loud and out loud?

> Praise Him with loud cymbals;
> Praise Him with clashing cymbals!
>   (Psalm 150:5).

The Psalm concludes with:

> Let everything that has breath praise the Lord.
> Praise the Lord! (Psalm 150:6).

The word for "praise" here is *halal* which means to shine; to make a show, to boast; and to be clamorously foolish. I don't think any of us come close to praising like that, but we should. When is the last time you were foolishly loud, boasting, and raving about God? That is the meaning of the word "hallelujah," to celebrate God clamorously.

Public and Private

Let me state clearly that the dynamics of public worship are dramatically different from those of private worship. Some expressions are great for private worship, but they can be distracting when done in public.

THE DYNAMICS OF PUBLIC WORSHIP ARE DRAMATICALLY DIFFERENT FROM THOSE OF PRIVATE WORSHIP.

In a public service, you should consider the Lord and others before yourself. It is a challenge not to be self-indulgent while keeping your worship authentic. Consider whether your expressions, especially if they are loud or involve movement, are appropriate to the context and respectful of the worship environment. Indeed, showing respect for others and obeying Scripture are a form of worship. Remember, Paul advises believers to:

> Seek to abound for the edification of the church. ... When you assemble ... Let all things be done for edification. ... But all things must

be done properly and in an orderly manner
(1 Corinthians 14:12, 26, 40 NASB).

Notice that all things—all forms of worship—are to be done for edification of the whole body.

Diverse

God enjoys diversity. The universe is diverse, with different colors, sounds, rhythms, seasons, and species of creatures. The Creator likes them all. In the same way, He likes diverse worship, with the blending of different personalities, peoples, cultures, styles, expressions, languages, and vocabularies.

There isn't a particular form, expression, or musical style that He prefers over another. However, Scripture mentions certain things that are especially pleasing to Him—like singing praise. He likes it all—your song and mine. He inhabits each personal, spontaneous, and vertical song. He receives it all, and so should we.

This is verified in heaven, where everything is perfect. Worship there is not robotic or cloned, with everyone worshipping the same way. They worship similarly but not identically, because there is diversity with every language, culture, and music present. Worship brings together God and people, heaven and earth, time and eternity, individual tastes and cultural styles.

To force people into the same worship expression makes them clones and creates a dishonest worship culture. If only one or two styles or expressions were acceptable to the Lord, He would have to apologize to all the cultures around the world and throughout history that have worshiped Him with different sounds and instruments. All worship to God is good if it is honest and sincere.

So you see, though we all have different methods of expressing our worship, affection for God is at the center of it all. Your passionate relationship with God is the spring from which your worship expressions flow. Let your love for God find new ways to express itself.

Study Guide

1. Why do you think that expressing your worship is sometimes awkward and hard to do?
2. What expressions of worship do you prefer?
3. What expressions are harder for you to use in your worship?
4. Are there expressions you would like to use in worship but for some reason do not use?
5. Do you feel free to worship in public? If so, why?
6. What ways do you worship privately but not in public?

Scripture and Reflection

Read 1 Corinthians 13 and Psalm 33
1. What are the main hindrances keeping you from expressing your worship to God?
2. Will your worship to the Lord be different as a result of contemplating the various ways you can worship? If so, in what new ways will you express your worship?

Prayer

Heavenly Father, You deserve the greatest and grandest worship. I know I have held back some of my worship of You. I want to worship in a way that pleases You. Empower me with your Holy Spirit to worship at a higher level of expression. I appreciate your patience with me as I endeavor to be more expressive in my worship. I love You with all that I am, and thank you for the amazing love that You have for me. In Jesus' name, Amen.

9

God Talk

He (Jesus) is the perfect worshipper,
knowing His Father uninterruptedly,
submissively, and completely.
—*Harold Best*

Have you ever wondered what God's thoughts are about worship? What kind of worship would please Him? Well, He has told us.

It was a long walk up the mountain for Isaac. They had been climbing for a while, and the load of wood he had strapped over his back was getting heavy.

Father said we were going up the mountain to worship. Isaac replayed in his mind the conversation his father and the servants had.

I wonder where we will offer the sacrifice.

Wait a minute! We don't have a sacrifice! Puzzled, Isaac pondered what they would give God in worship. *Father is such a devout worshipper, I'm sure he has something in mind.*

Isaac didn't know that God had spoken to his father, Abraham, to sacrifice Isaac as an offering to God. That is what the worshippers of the savage demon gods do. They burn their children alive to appease the dark spirits. What is happening here? Why would God say that?

I know Father has a plan, Isaac reasoned to himself.

He has such absolute trust in God. If he doesn't have a plan, then God does. Isaac continued the ascent of Mount Mariah.

Isaac finally spoke up: "Father."

"Yes, my son," Abraham replied.

"You have the fire and I have the wood, but where is the lamb to burn for the sacrifice?" Isaac knew that God had asked his father to make a burnt offering to Him on this mountain. He also knew that the right sacrifice was to be a lamb. But he didn't see a lamb.

"God will provide the lamb for the sacrifice," Abraham said. What faith! Did he really know there would be a lamb when they arrived? Or, was he hiding his intent from his son?

"Son, we must obey God! It doesn't matter what He asks. Always remember to do as he says. He knows what is best for us." Abraham was mentoring Isaac. He wanted him to understand what was taking place.

When they reached the place God had told him, Abraham built a stone altar, and Isaac put the wood on it.

"Stand still, son!" Abraham said. "Don't struggle. I am going to tie your hands. Okay?"

"Yes, Father."

Abraham took the rope that had bound the wood and tied Isaac's hands in front of him.

"Father, I am scared!"

"We are giving of ourselves in worship to God."

"But why aren't your hands tied? I don't want to do this!" Isaac said as he moved away from Abraham.

"Come, son! We must obey God!"

ABRAHAM GRABBED HIS SON, LAID HIM ON THE ALTAR, AND QUICKLY REACHED FOR THE KNIFE.

After a little scuffle, Abraham grabbed his son, laid him on the altar, and quickly reached for the knife before Isaac could roll off the altar and escape.

"Son, close your eyes and lie still!" Abraham said, as he raised the knife into the air to plunge it into his son's chest.

Just in time an angel manifested and yelled out, "Abraham! Abraham!"

"I'm here!"

"Don't touch your son! Now I know that you fear God because you did what He asked you, even though it might have cost you your son."

"Look!" The angel pointed. Abraham looked up and saw a ram stuck by his horn in the bushes. He took the animal and prepared to offer it to God in the place of his son.

Isaac rolled off the altar and used his teeth to get the rope off his hands. "Father, let me help."

Later that afternoon, as the sacrifice was smoldering, Abraham said, "Son, we will call this place 'The Lord Has Provided.'"

"Father, that is perfect."

Suddenly they heard a loud voice: "I swear by Myself that, because you worshipped in obedience and did not hold back your son, I will bless your descendants and make them as numerous as sand on a beach or stars in the sky. You will overtake your enemies and spoil their possessions.

Through your relatives all the nations of the earth will be blessed because you obeyed Me."

Abraham and Isaac fell to the ground and bowed ever so low in deep gratitude.

Later, it quickly became a common saying, "On the mountain of the Lord it will be provided." Abraham's worship had changed both his life and the world from that point on.

God Teaches Worship

The very first time the Holy Spirit mentions worship in Scripture is in this story in Genesis:

> Now it came to pass after these things that God tested Abraham, and said to him, ... "Take now your son, your only *son* Isaac, whom you love, and go to the land of Moriah, and offer him there as a burnt offering on one of the mountains of which I shall tell you." (Genesis 22:1–2).

God's request was very difficult: kill your son as a sacrifice to Him. You would think this is contrary to God's nature to have someone kill another person, for didn't God say to Moses, "You shall not kill?"

But look at Abraham's response:

> Then on the third day Abraham lifted his eyes and saw the place afar off. And Abraham said to his young men, "Stay here with the donkey; the

lad and I will go yonder and worship, and we
will come back to you" (Genesis 22:4–5).

Some people think that worship is singing a slow song.
What was Abraham really saying here? "The boy and I will
go yonder and sing a slow song"? Obviously that was not
what he was saying. In Abraham's story there is a key to
God's thoughts on worship. Let's read on:

And Abraham stretched out his hand and
took the knife to slay his son. But the Angel of
the Lord called to him from heaven and said,
"Abraham, Abraham!" So he said, "Here I am."
And He said, "Do not lay your hand on the lad,
or do anything to him; for now I know that you
fear God, since you have not withheld your son,
your only *son*, from Me" (Genesis 22:10–12).

In the Old Testament, sacrifices had to be the best that
people had. Abraham offered the best he had—his beloved
son. Acceptable sacrifices couldn't have a blemish. God
delights in pure sacrifices. You and I must give God our first
and our best in obedience, even when we don't understand
our circumstances.

Abraham obeyed God and was willing to do all that He
said. Abraham demonstrated strong faith in God, knowing
He would somehow provide. God is pleased with the sacrifices we make for Him and others.

Through him then let us continually offer up
a sacrifice of praise to God, that is, the fruit

of lips that acknowledge his name. Do not
neglect to do good and to share what you
have, for such sacrifices are pleasing to God
(Hebrews 13:15–16 ESV).

Worship involves sacrifice and obedience. Someone once said, "The highest praise is not worship, but obedience." John Piper says, "Through Christ two things become worshipful sacrifices in our life: the fruit of lips that acknowledge his name [worth]; ... singing and praying and repenting and confession, and secondly, the fruit of deeds."[1] Don't forget to worship by sacrificing what you want and obeying God. It pleases Him. When we obey God He is honored and esteemed through our actions and attitude of obedience."

God said to Abraham, "Now I know that you fear God." Your worship must have the fear—deep reverence and respect—of the Lord. When you are too casual in your attitude toward God, your worship isn't what it should be. Come before Him and:

Offer to God pleasing service *and* acceptable
worship, with modesty *and* pious care and
godly fear *and* awe; For our God [is indeed] a
consuming fire (Hebrews 12:28–29 AMPCE).

Jesus Teaches Worship

John, a young disciple of Jesus, quoted what Jesus taught about worship to a woman in Samaria:

> The time is coming—it has, in fact, come—
> when what you're called will not matter and
> where you go to worship will not matter.
>
> It's who you are and the way you live that
> count before God. Your worship must engage
> your spirit in the pursuit of truth. That's the kind
> of people the Father is out looking for: those who
> are simply and honestly *themselves* before him
> in their worship (John 4:22–23 MSG).

You might be more familiar with the phrase,

> God *is* Spirit, and those who worship Him must
> worship in spirit and truth (John 4:24).

Jesus taught these two simple principles—worship in spirit and in truth. He emphasized that worship should involve your spirit and the Holy Spirit. If it doesn't, you probably are not worshipping. So many people think that they have worshipped if they sang the song the worship leader leads. Worship is not a singing a song, a production of music, or a service. Worship is "the response of God's Spirit in us to that Spirit in Him, whereby we answer 'Abba, Father,' while the deep things of our spirit call out unto the deep things of God's Spirit."[2]

True worshippers are those who truly and sincerely worship God—those who worship with the heart and not merely in form or external action.

True means the real deal. It is the genuine, as opposed to the fake or the pretend. You can be a false worshipper if you are not worshipping truthfully and honestly.

The phrase *in spirit* does not mean the order of service, ceremony, or any external worship. It refers to the engagement of the heart, the soul, and the mind. It involves our spirit and God's Spirit.

When Jesus says *in truth* He is talking about being real. It comes from a root word meaning "to not conceal." Genuine worshippers are honest in their worship. They don't pretend or act or perform. True worshippers don't act differently on the platform than they do at home. Acting is subduing the real under the pretend. Guard yourself against being a performer or actor in worship. Remember, in worship God does not read your external art but your internal heart.

IN WORSHIP GOD DOES NOT READ YOUR EXTERNAL ART BUT YOUR INTERNAL HEART.

Jesus gives us two reasons why this kind of worship should take place. First, the Father seeks it—He looks for it and desires it from you. Second, He is giving us a new order of worship. Jesus abolished the external emphasis on actions, forms, and liturgies. The Father wants spiritual worship and real worship.

The Perfect Worshipper

Have you ever considered worship in the life of Jesus? He worshipped the Father almost all the time—praying and praising Him constantly. There were many instances of worship around Jesus' birth. For example, when Mary greeted Elizabeth, who was pregnant with John, the baby danced in Elizabeth's womb. Mary continued in worship by singing a beautiful prophetic song—the Magnificat.

Another instance of worship at the birth of Jesus is the shepherds praising at the visitation of the army of angels who descended out of heaven singing their worship. Then there were the wise men from the East who came and worshipped Jesus. Also, when Jesus was brought into the temple to be dedicated, Simeon and Anna worshipped God in spontaneous song.

As Jesus grew he continued to model a life of worship. Often, before a meal, He would eulogize or give thanks for the food. When He became more public in His ministry, He led His disciples in singing songs of worship.

> Then they sang a hymn and went out to the
> Mount of Olives (Matt 26:30 NLT).

As an effective leader and mentor, Jesus modeled worship to His disciples. Luke recounts when Jesus worshipped expressively and extravagantly, outwardly expressing praise and joy to His Father:

> At that very time He rejoiced greatly in the
> Holy Spirit, and said, "I praise You, O Father,
> Lord of heaven and earth" (Luke 10:21 NASB).

The word *rejoice* in this verse means "to jump for exceeding joy." Very possibly, Jesus leapt or danced right in front of His disciples, and then broke out in a spontaneous outburst of praise to His Father. Jesus was not pious, conservative, or religious. Jesus generously expressed His free-flowing worship to His Father in heaven.

Jesus worshipped extravagantly and expressively, and He encouraged others to worship the same way. Jesus strongly opposed religious leaders who wanted to shut down the exuberant and expressive worship of His followers.

JESUS STRONGLY OPPOSED RELIGIOUS LEADERS WHO WANTED TO SHUT DOWN THE EXUBERANT AND EXPRESSIVE WORSHIP OF HIS FOLLOWERS.

> Then, as He was now drawing near the descent of the Mount of Olives, the whole multitude of the disciples began to rejoice and praise God with a loud voice for all the mighty works they had seen, saying:
>
> "'Blessed *is* the King who comes in the name of the Lord!'
>
> Peace in heaven and glory in the highest!"
>
> And some of the Pharisees called to Him from the crowd, "Teacher, rebuke Your disciples."
>
> But He answered and said to them, "I tell you that if these should keep silent, the stones would immediately cry out" (Luke 19:37–40.)

Jesus opposed restrictions that religious leaders put on sincere, spontaneous worship. It was as if He was saying, "If the redeemed won't praise God loud and long, the mineral world will." Or perhaps He was saying, "If these sincere worshippers will be quiet, then you will hear the stones sing out! God will have exuberant and expressive worship!"

Apostle Paul

Paul, inspired by the Spirit of God, also encouraged the new believers in Philippi in their worship:

> We ... worship God in the Spirit, rejoice in Christ Jesus, and have no confidence in the flesh (Philippians 3:3).

In describing how to worship, it is interesting that Paul makes no mention of music, art, or the order of service. He says that we worship in the Spirit. It is very important to note that both Jesus and Paul emphasize the spirituality of worship. Therein is a key to true worship.

You are to worship in and by the Holy Spirit. Worship is to be supernatural—beyond the natural realm of the art and actions of man. Your spirit and the Holy Spirit must be involved in your worship. The focus is not on your outward actions but on inner attitudes.

The Holy Spirit helps and facilitates your worship. This is much more than a formal program of planned and produced elements called a worship service. They are the tools and helps of worship, but they themselves are not worship. We most certainly can worship outwardly in a planned worship service as long as your heart and spirit are involved and your affection is real and sincere, just as Jesus taught.

Study Guide

1. How do you describe true worship?
2. What important aspects of worship did Jesus emphasize?
3. How do you worship "in the Spirit?"
4. What practical habits and attitudes in your life can cause your worship to become more spiritual?
5. What does it mean to you to be real in worship?
6. How will you make planned or structured worship more spiritual?

Scripture and Reflection

Read Genesis 22:1–18 and John 4:1–26
1. How do you think having God's Spirit occupy your spirit will change your worship?
2. In what ways has your worship been more superficial than spiritual?
3. In what are you confident when you worship?
4. What will you do to make your worship more honest?
5. What will you do to allow the Holy Spirit to have a greater place in your life and in your worship?

Prayer

Heavenly Father, Thank You for instructing me how to worship. I desire my worship to be real, honest, and pleasing to You. Help me not to act or pretend when I worship You. Show me how to worship in and with Your Holy Spirit. Teach me to worship in spirit and truth, putting no confidence in my abilities or preparation. In Jesus' name, Amen.

10

DNA

When I worship, I would rather my heart be without
words than my words be without heart.
—*LaMar Boschman*

All true worship is in essence a matter of the heart.
—*John Piper*

The lab was busy this day. Technicians scurried everywhere. There had been what they thought was a release of deadly chemicals in downtown Miami. Homeland security was involved. All law enforcement and first responders wanted to know what they were dealing with.

This was the lab for CSI: Miami. The technicians were tasked with the responsibility to determine what chemicals were used and if they were deadly. They were busy doing chemical tests, filling beakers, and checking the facts based on evidence.

What is the chemical composition of the mist and the residue that they found? That was the question they had to answer. What is this stuff? The question was on everyone's mind. The media had opinions and were not afraid to share their suspicions, which caused some people to panic.

Politicians and activists started spontaneous rallies, social media posts, and interviews just hours after it happened. Almost everyone was saying that this was a terrible thing and it should not be allowed. Why didn't the government do more to protect us? Everyone had an opinion and made a judgment without any solid evidence. They were proclaiming things that were only speculation.

It wasn't long before the lab determined that the substance was not harmful. The proper examination of the chemical composition showed that the public was not in any danger.

BUT DID ANY WORSHIP REALLY OCCUR?

Do you realize that something like this is what happens in worship? Everyone has an opinion. Worship is this and worship is that. We make incorrect assumptions of what is worship. It seems as if everyone is declaring, "Wow, what a great worship service!" The congregation believes it, the pastor proclaims it, and later it shows up on social media. But did any worship really occur?

What about having a WSI, a worship scene investigation, to see if the worship we experience is real? We must examine the composition of the worship that occurred to determine if it is sincere and real. This process will train you in what to look for when you worship. It will also help you as a leader facilitate authentic worship, because is has its own composition or DNA.

Broad and Narrow

To begin with, we must understand that there is a broad aspect to worship and also a narrower one. Worship in a broad sense includes your attitude to the Lord. It is the way you live your life, conduct yourself at work, witness to someone, or visit the sick. Worship could include singing and playing music for the Lord, but it is not limited to that. All these are indirect acts of worship and find expression in the adoration and affection of your Savior. These are more broad definitions of worship and, though they are in some measure real, they are perhaps not as intimate and personal.

However, in a more narrow sense, worship is more personal. It is the vertical expression of your heart's attitude when it is directed straight to God. You may publicly sing and play music and not even think of the Lord, and some would call it worship. However, when your heart connects with God, at that moment you are directly worshipping Him with your singing and playing.

So, from that perspective, let's explore the essential, non-negotiable aspects of worship—the DNA of the fundamental elements of the more intimate and more spiritual worship.

Get Real

In the fundamental and narrower definition, worship is not heartlessly singing your favorite songs. Worship is

WHEN YOUR LIPS DON'T MATCH YOUR HEART, THERE IS NO WORSHIP. beyond form and outward actions. When your lips don't match your heart, there is no worship. Jesus was painfully honest when He said,

> These people ... honor Me with *their* lips,
> But their heart is far from Me.
> And in vain they worship Me (Matthew 15:8–9).

Another way to say it is if you don't mean what you sing your worship is not genuine.

Attitude in the Action

The essence of worship is not natural but supernatural. Worship is not an external activity but an internal activity. Worship is an organic attitude long before it becomes an expressive action. It is not a practiced art but a prayed attitude. Worship is not action-formed but attitude-formed.

To say it another way, it is your attitude in your action that makes what you do worship. For example, for a dancer it is the devotion in the motion that makes the person's movement worship. Otherwise it is just an art form or a dance performance. The act of dancing is not itself worship, but rather an expression of worship. Devotion must be in your heart to make your dance movements worship to God.

If you play a musical instrument, worship is what you pray in what you play. It is engaging your spirit and heart cry through the expression of playing your guitar, keyboard, or drums. You mean what you play with attitude toward God.

The same principle applies to singing. When your spirit cries out to God in your singing, you are worshipping. Your groan in your tone is what makes your songs worship. The cry, or sigh, in the act of singing is what empowers the song to be spiritual and worshipful. Worship is to put meaning into your singing.

You also can apply this to lifting your hands. Just because you lift your hands in the air during a worship service does not mean you are worshipping. It is when you lift your hands with your heart that gives your lifted hands meaning and makes that expression become worship.

> Let us lift our hearts and hands
> To God in heaven (Lamentations 3:41).

Heart Issues

Your heart and your spirit are the genesis of true, spiritual worship. If worship is not in your heart, it is not in your art. Worship must be in your heart to be real and authentic. It keeps your worship from being pretend or pretense, which Jesus labeled as hypocrisy when He said, "These

IF WORSHIP IS NOT IN YOUR HEART, IT IS NOT IN YOUR ART.

worshipers are frauds, trying to impress each other by saying the right things but their heart isn't in it. They pretend they are worshiping me, but they don't mean it" (Matt 15:8-9).

You must mean what you do when it comes to worship, whether it is singing, speaking, playing, or praying. In the spiritual acts of worship it is essential for your spirit to be involved. That way your real heart cry and sincere intent is present, making your expression sincere.

You can have inward attitude without the outward action and be worshipping. But you cannot do the outward actions of worship without inward attitude and have true worship. What gives our worship integrity is the condition of our heart, not the condition of our art. Another way to say it is that *worship is not the sound of music but the sound of the heart.*

Horizontal and Vertical

Just as there are songs written about God and songs written to God, so praise can be about God or to God. You can honor God either directly or indirectly. And so it is in worship that you can express yourself to Him directly or indirectly. When you address the audience of One directly, you're expressing your heart to Him personally and intimately. When you speak or sing of Him indirectly, it still honors or praises Him, but is not as personal and intimate. One is horizontal and the other is vertical.

For example, I can speak to others about my wife, praising her beauty and character. This would be expressing adoration indirectly. But it is not until I focus on her, look into her eyes, and express my love directly to her, that I truly express my love to her.

Directing your affection to God and focusing spiritually on Him is essential in intimate worship. If you look only out and not up you miss greater levels of intimacy with God. One is primarily impersonal and functional and you probably will not develop greater relationship with God. However, adoration and affection focused directly to God will cause personal interaction and deepen your relationship with God.

Performance Issues

It is correct to conclude playing music for people is not necessarily worship. Likewise, singing from the large screens in the front of a church is not necessarily worship either, though people wrongly assume because they sang what they were given, they have worshipped. Perhaps it is only karaoke.

Consider this comparison chart below that contrasts worship and performance. Keep in mind the terms are loose generalizations. However, they help you see the unique contrast.

True worship is more organic than systematic, more prophetic than produced, more mystical than methodical, more mysterious than manufactured, and more relational than rational. Planning, producing, and practicing a service does not create worship unless hearts connect to the Lord during the activity and action.

PERFORMANCE	WORSHIP
External	Internal
Horizontal	Vertical
Natural	Spiritual
For man	For God
Art focused	Heart focused
Mechanical	Relational
Play-ful	Prayer-ful
Organized	Organic
Form	Faith
Produced	Prophetic
Complex	Simple

Different From Praise

Another way to look at the DNA of worship is to differentiate it from praise. Worship and praise are not exactly the same thing. Worship is somewhat different from praise in several ways. For example the Bible talks about a sacrifice of praise being an audible action whereas the sacrifice of worship is an attitude acted out. An example of worship acted out is presenting our bodies as a living sacrifice to God by obeying Him as Abraham did.

Another difference is you can proclaim declarations of praise in faith despite your circumstances, but when you worship, you must mean it. The sacrifice of praise is the fruit of your lips, but worship is the fruit of your heart.

> Therefore by Him let us continually offer
> the sacrifice of praise to God, that is, the
> fruit of our lips, giving thanks to His name
> (Hebrews 13:15).

Worship is about attitude, love, affection, and adoration. Praise is about sacrifice, proclamation, and declaration. You can have a proud heart and still proclaim the greatness of God. But you cannot come near to the Lord to worship with a hard and proud spirit because:

> God resists the proud, but gives grace to the
> humble. (James 4:6).

Motives

Since worship is so much about the heart, your motives play a big role in determining whether your worship is honest or not. Occasionally you should ask yourself, "Why do I have my hands raised?" Sometimes you may be doing it out of habit, or because everyone else is. Perhaps you are thinking about where you are going to eat after the service. At the moment you have that thought, you are not worshipping anymore, because your heart is not focused on the Lord. As humans, we are easily distracted causing us to vacillate and often go in and out of worship.

Have you ever seen a person go to the front of the congregation to express their worship and sensed that something about them was not quite right? They give themselves away when they look back to see if someone is watching them. I enjoy seeing young people flood to the front to worship God as a group. But when it is only one person perhaps you wondered, like me, about their motives. Perhaps you have thought to yourself, "If their worship is for the Lord, why didn't they go to the back and express themselves to Him? God can see them anywhere. Are they up here to be noticed?"

Keep in mind that only the Lord sees your heart and knows your true motives. You can only assess another's worship by discerning from outward appearance, and your discernment may not always be accurate. All of us need to be careful to not judge the worship experience of others. Each of us is accountable for our own worship, not for other people's worship. However, as a leader you can discern.

Heart Fragrance

Did you know that, because worship comes from within you, your spirit could taint or color your worship? Your spirit is the atmosphere of your heart. Sometimes that atmosphere smells bad because of the pollution of sin, negative attitudes, or self-centeredness. When your heart offers up worship to God, the aroma of your heart goes with it, so your spirit can fog up both your inside and outside. Likewise, your spirit can color your worship.

WHEN YOUR HEART OFFERS UP WORSHIP TO GOD, THE AROMA OF YOUR HEART GOES WITH IT.

Conversely, if you have prayed, fasted, and read God's Word allowing it to wash you before you worship, your spirit may have a pleasant and fragrant atmosphere. Those spiritual disciplines cause transparency that allows the Holy Spirit to be seen and sensed in you.

Did you remember a time when you heard a musician sing, and you sensed the Holy Spirit? You might have called the musician "anointed." What you might have been sensing is the spirit and essence of a worshipper who had a soft and pliable heart. That kind of heart comes from being in the presence of God. The atmosphere of their spirit is infused with the fragrance of a sweet and sincere heart that allowed you to sense the presence of the Holy Spirit.

It is critical to the integrity of worship to know what the true DNA of worship is. It will keep your worship pure and honest.

Study Guide

1. How would you describe the DNA of worship?
2. How do you check your sincerity and motives when you worship?
3. How can you tell if your worship is vertical?
4. What did the author say makes a person anointed?
5. What do you think a musician or a worshipper should do if they fall into a performance attitude when it's time to lead worship?
6. Do you find it hard to keep your focus on the Lord during a time of worship?

Scripture and Reflection

Read Psalm 1, Psalm 19, and James 4

1. What are some things about performance that you struggle with?
2. What is easier for you— focusing vertically or horizontally—focusing on God or on other people? Why?
3. What personal habits or activities have hindered you in living a pure, worshipful life to the Lord?
4. In what ways will you refocus your heart and your life in order to offer God a pure life of worship?

Prayer

Heavenly Father, You are a most gracious and loving God. I want my worship to be pleasing to you. I want to have the heart and spirit of a true worshipper. Convict me of my habits and attitudes that pollute my spirit. I will be quick to repent and change the atmosphere of my heart. I want my spirit to be pure and fragrant before You. Let my heart have the DNA of true, spiritual worship. In Jesus' name, Amen.

11

Celestial

I believe that angels have the capacity to employ
heavenly celestial music. In heaven we will be taught
the language and music of the celestial world.
—*Billy Graham*

John looked up from the floor when he heard the guard
push the wooden plate under his cell door. The bread
was stale and moldy, but that is what prisoners get—the
leftovers. He quickly devoured it, and the pain in his stomach eased. Life was hard and cruel in prison.

He laid his head back on the straw and recalled what had
happened to him. Yesterday had been a hard day of work.
The Roman guards were relentlessly making this Christian
pastor suffer.

*It is difficult to cut the volcanic rock with just a chisel when
you are eighty years old,* he thought to himself. His feet were
bleeding and sore. There are no sandals for prisoners on the
island of Patmos. His sackcloth didn't keep him very warm
in this dark, dank dungeon.

His thoughts went back to what he had experienced that
night. He replayed the vision he had. It took his attention
away from his pain and suffering. He had seen and heard

something most unusual and very mysterious—the music of the celestial world.

Was I dreaming? John asked himself, *or did I go there? I don't really know. However, I know that what I saw struck me to my core. I don't really know.*

John recalled the details of his spiritual trance. He saw an open door and heard a voice saying, "Come up where I am and I'll show you things."

He reached for the parchment he had hidden from the guards and mumbled, "I have to write this down."

John wrote:

"I saw a white throne and One seated in regal majesty. There were hues of amber and emerald around the regal chair and twenty-four thrones with twenty-four earthly leaders crowned with gold and dressed in brilliant white.

"There were four creatures unlike anything I've ever seen. They were alien-like; not from earth's domain, but occupants of the spiritual realm. The sound of their singing was unusual. These four-headed, six-winged, multi-eyed aliens sang without a break, 'Holy, holy, holy is the Lord God Almighty, Who was and is and is to come!'

THESE FOUR-HEADED, SIX-WINGED, MULTI-EYED ALIENS SANG WITHOUT A BREAK.

"I was overcome with the majestic power of their song. I had barely recovered when I heard others began to sing. The twenty-four earthly leaders got off their thrones and bowed their heads to the ground before the One on the great white throne. Suddenly, they took their crowns off and threw them violently before the throne, erupting in song, singing, 'You are worthy, O God to receive all glory, honor and power.'

"Again, I was overwhelmed. My body grew limp, and I fell to the ground and sobbed at what I had witnessed."

Perfectly Pristine

When exploring the mysteries of worship, it is important to consider what worship is like in the celestial realm. In heaven worship is continual and is absolute perfection. Worship before God's throne is just like He wants it to be.

Worship in heaven is not influenced or affected by the passions and preferences of earthlings. The presence of the evil one, the proliferation of sin, and the curse on the earth and mankind have no effect on worship in this heavenly realm. Worship rises genuine and pure from the affectionate hearts of angels and the redeemed. This adoration flows from these celestial bodies in expressions that are exquisite and perfectly appropriate.

The Seat and the Sheep

There are people throughout history who have seen a glimpse of heaven and have described what they saw and heard. John, the youngest disciple of Jesus, is one of those. While he was imprisoned on the island of Patmos, he had a vision which he described in the book of Revelation.

John said he looked up and noted a door standing open in heaven. A voice told him, "Come up here, and I will show you things" (Revelation 4:1).

The first thing John saw was a throne. In heaven—up front and center—is not a worship artist, nor a worship leader, a pastor, or any Christian leader. There is simply a throne and a Lamb nearby—a seat and a sheep.

> Immediately I was in the Spirit; and behold, a
>   throne set in heaven,
> and *One* sat on the throne (Revelation 4:2).

This sovereign seat is the center of everything: heaven and earth, time and eternity, all space and infinity, all things past, present, and future. It is on this highly esteemed chair that all things focus. All roads of earthlings and angels end at the throne of the Almighty. All songs of the terrestrial and the celestial will be for the One on this throne.

On the throne sits the Lord of heaven and earth—your heavenly Father— limitless in power, perfect in knowledge, and ceaseless in creativity. The worship before the throne is not about men and their musical art. All artists, dancers, musicians, singers, and leaders will fall face down before the Omnipotent Potentate, breathless with what they see and hear of Him. A little later in the book, John describes Jesus as a Lamb and notes His proximity to the throne.

The throne and the Lamb should always be in the middle of your worship and the central focus of your worship. It is critical that the great Sovereign One and His Son are at the center of our lyrics, our prayers, and our sermons. God is the focal point of all our worship.

Celestial Songs

No single worship style is favored over another in heaven. There is no debate over the preferences of worshippers. No one there says, "Why don't we sing more hymns?" or "I don't like those songs!" In heaven, there are no worship wars with stubborn hearts vying for attention or promoting their preferences and tastes. Only One sits on the throne, and what He wants will be done.

IN HEAVEN THERE IS A MULTIPLICITY OF MUSIC BECAUSE GOD DELIGHTS IN DIVERSITY.

In heaven there is a multiplicity of music because God delights in diversity. He is about variety, not about sameness. We know there are many styles of music in heaven because John wrote what he saw and heard:

> A great multitude which no one could number, of all nations, tribes, peoples, and tongues, standing before the throne and before the Lamb, clothed with white robes (Revelation 7:9).

As he continued to describe the worship in heaven, John mentions the kind of songs that he heard:

> And I saw ... those who have the victory
> over the beast. ... sing the song of Moses, the
> servant of God, and the song of the Lamb
> (Revelation 15:2–3).

It is not clear if the lyrics that follow are from the song of Moses or the song of the Lamb. Some scholars say that they are the same song. Nevertheless, the lyrics of the song are:

> Great and marvelous *are* Your works,
> Lord God Almighty!
> Just and true *are* Your ways,
> O King of the saints! (Revelation 15:3).

Interestingly, there is a certain kind of song that is perpetually sung in heaven. It is called the *new song*.

> They sang as it were a new song before the
> throne, before the four living creatures,
> and the elders; and no one could learn that
> song except the hundred *and* forty-four
> thousand (Revelation 14:3).

These new songs are spontaneous songs that have never been sung before. As the worshippers in heaven behold the pristine perfection of God they reflect it back in fresh, instantaneous musical expressions. The new song is an original song—a kind of song not heard before or known prior.

Celestial Musicians

ALMOST EVERYONE IN HEAVEN IS A MUSICIAN, PLAYING AND SINGING WORSHIP TO GOD.

Almost everyone in heaven is a musician, playing and singing worship to God. The Scriptures reveal that not only the hundred and forty-four thousand play and sing, but also do the four living creatures, the twenty-four elders, all the overcomers, and all the angels of God.

I saw *something* like a sea of glass mingled with fire, and those who have the victory over the beast, over his image and over his mark *and* over the number of his name, standing on the sea of glass, having harps of God (Revelation 15:2).

Now when He had taken the scroll, the four living creatures and the twenty-four elders fell down before the Lamb, each having a harp. ... And they sang a new song (Revelation 5:8–9).

Celestial Instruments

In heaven, instruments of music are played before the throne of God. However, they are a certain kind of instrument. John says,

> I heard a voice from heaven, like the voice of
> many waters, and like the voice of loud thun-
> der. And I heard the sound of harpists playing
> their harps (Revelation 14:2).

The musical instruments John heard repeatedly were stringed instruments. It is interesting that there is no mention of percussion or wind instruments used in worship in heaven. John heard and saw trumpets; however, they were not used in worship. They were announcing the judgments of God. In connection with worship, the Bible clearly mentions that almost everyone in heaven plays a stringed instrument.

Order of Worship

John also described the position of the worshippers as they played and sang. It was almost like they were in many round stadiums stacked on top of each other, only larger and more glorious than earthly arenas:

> Then I looked, and I heard the voice of many
> angels around the throne, the living creatures,
> and the elders; and the number of them was
> ten thousand times ten thousand, and thou-
> sands of thousands (Revelation 5:11).

The number of angels was so numerous that John used the largest number in the Greek numerical system—ten thousand times ten thousand. In other words, it was incalculable.

Scholars suppose they stood all around, above, and possibly below the throne of God singing His praises.

> Around the throne *were* twenty-four thrones,
> and on the thrones I saw twenty-four elders
> sitting, clothed in white robes; ... Seven lamps
> of fire *were* burning before the throne. ...
> Before the throne *there was* a sea of glass, like
> crystal. And in the midst of the throne, and
> around the throne, *were* four living creatures
> (Revelation 4:4–6).

The four living creatures (symbolizing leadership) worshipped before the throne. Behind or near them were the twenty-four elders, and behind them an incalculable number of angels. In front of the throne, spread the crystal sea full of worship musicians. It is such a large group of stringed-instrument players that they cannot be counted; all are playing and singing to the audience of One.

Modes of Worship

The expressions of the worshippers in heaven are extreme. There is constant action of obeisance to the One who sits on the throne.

> The twenty-four elders fall down before Him
> who sits on the throne and worship Him who
> lives forever and ever, and cast their crowns
> before the throne (Revelation 4:10).

Not only do they fall upon the ground in humble reverence, but also they throw their crowns at the foot of the throne.

When you come to worship, you lay all your trophies of accomplishment, victory, and success at the feet of Jesus. You come by no merit of your own. You come acknowledging Yahweh as the supreme King. All lesser kings of His dominion bow in obeisance to Him and lay the symbols of their reign at His feet.

They know that all their authority and blessings come from Him. None of us have enough merit or virtue to come and minister before Him. We simply lay it all down in total submission to the Ruler of heaven and earth. This act of obeisance continues endlessly in the celestial realm.

The other dynamic about worship in heaven is that it is loud and long. If that does not sit well with you, ponder these two things. First, you will not be in your current earthly suit, or body, but you will have a celestial suit that has different capacities and abilities. You will be able to create and hear sound differently than you do now. For example, you will be able to sing for a thousand years and not have to sleep or refuel.

Second, everyone else will also be singing loud and long. If you don't, you will stick out, and it might be a bit embarrassing.

This is what John heard in heaven:

> Then I looked, and I heard the voice of many
> angels around the throne, the living crea-
> tures, and the elders; and the number of them
> was ten thousand times ten thousand, and

thousands of thousands, saying with a loud
voice:

"Worthy is the Lamb who was slain
To receive power and riches and wisdom,
And strength and honor and glory and blessing!
(Revelation 5:11–12).

Scholars say that the phrases in quotations in the book of Revelation are called songs because of the nature of the address to God. Most of the passages that refer to speaking can be singing, especially when alluding to angelic beings. However, the word for speaking is consistent with singing, so we can regard it as such.[1]

Again John described the voluminous worship:

I looked, and behold, a great multitude which
no one could number, of all nations, tribes,
peoples, and tongues, standing before the
throne and before the Lamb, clothed with
white robes, with palm branches in their
hands, and crying out with a loud voice, saying,
"Salvation *belongs* to our God who sits on
the throne, and to the Lamb!" All the angels
stood around the throne and the elders and
the four living creatures, and fell on their
faces before the throne and worshiped God
(Revelation 7:9–11).

Note, these worshippers were clothed in white—symbolic of their purity. The blood of the Lamb cleansed them.

You and I must approach our Lord with repentant hearts, asking Him to cleanse us from our sins.

Everyone before the throne falls prostrate to honor and worship the great Sovereign—the Lord Almighty.

Study Guide

1. How is worship in heaven different from that on earth?

2. How would you describe worship in heaven to a person you don't know?

3. How should worship on earth be like the worship in heaven?

4. Name some songs that have phrases like the songs in heaven?

5. Whatever your role is in worship, what can you do to better align yourself with the worship described in heaven?

Scripture and Reflection

Read Revelation 4, 5, and 15

1. In what ways has your worship been more focused on temporary things than on eternal truths?

2. What specific ways will you change to make worship more like that in heaven?

3. How will knowing the way worship takes place in heaven impact you and the way you worship from now on?

Prayer

Heavenly Father, when I look into Your Word and see glimpses of heaven, I see worship that is perfect and transcendent, and I realize how my worship falls short of what it could be. I ask for Your help in making my worship more like that in heaven. I pray Your kingdom come and Your will be done in my heart as it is in heaven. Holy Spirit, touch my life and heart. Make my worship more like the worship of heaven. In Jesus' name, Amen.

12

Revealed

Worship is about an encounter—
coming into God's presence.
—*Jack Hayford*

He appeared in the same place He always had every day at sunset and began His stroll through the garden. His movement was ominous and powerful.

Adam heard it. "Quick, let's hide!" he warned.

The voice rang out through the dense tropical vegetation. "Where are you?"

"Eve, Let's hide here!"

They scurried behind a group of trees.

"Adam!" The voice echoed again. "Where are you?"

"Shhhh. ... Quiet!" Adam whispered to his wife, putting his finger over his lips. "He is coming."

He always came to visit about this time each day and they would converse and share their thoughts. They had always enjoyed relationship and interaction. It had brought each of them such happiness and fondness for one another. Today was different. Something was wrong.

"Adam, why are you hiding?" He inquired. He already knew but wanted Adam to say it. "You are behind the trees, aren't you?"

Adam and Eve had taken cover from His face behind the trees in the lush garden. They did not want to get close to Him or see Him. They separated themselves from Him and withdrew.

"Why are you running from My presence?" He asked.

They had never done this before. When He appeared they would run to meet Him, excited about their next encounter with their best friend. He had taken such good care of them and the garden. Everything was perfect and just as it should be. There was nothing wrong, unsatisfying, or out of place. When they thought of Him they would smile.

"I see you behind the trees," He said. "Come out!"

"We are naked!" For the first time Adam and Eve had realized their need for covering. Now their nakedness seemed inappropriate. They were ashamed.

The serpent dragon tempted them to eat fruit from the tree in the middle of the garden—the only tree God had forbidden them to eat. God said if they ate it, they would die.

However, when they ate the fruit of the tree, they could see what they had never noticed before. Their perspective became skewed, and they saw things incorrectly.

They realized they were naked. It had never bothered them before. So they dealt with this first problem by tying leaves from the vegetation together to hide themselves. It didn't concern them too much until He appeared.

"Who told you that you were naked? Here!" He had killed an animal, skinned it, and cured the hide. It seemed like He did it in an instant. Then He covered Adam and Eve's nakedness with the skin of an animal that was sacrificed for them.

"What have you done?" He asked. He knew the answer to that, but wanted to register that their disobedience had consequences.

"So that you will not eat of the tree of life, you are banished from My presence."

It was a very, very sad moment when Adam and his wife left the fertile forest of His plentiful provision. They had to vacate the spot where they encountered Him—where they visited and communed.

Adam's head hung down as he walked into the dust of a new world in which he would have to work hard just to provide for themselves.

"What just happened?" he asked Eve. "This is difficult to believe. Will we ever see Him again?"

To keep Adam from returning, mighty cherubs were commissioned to stand at the entrance to the spot where He revealed Himself. A flaming sword threatened anyone who would try to enter the presence again and eat of the tree of life. Man was now a fugitive from His presence. Like a fish out of water, he would eventually die.

The Secret

The secret is out: God has provided a way for man to return to His revealed presence. God misses the interaction and intimacy that He once had with Adam and E. The invitation is out:

Let us come before His presence with
thanksgiving;
Let us shout joyfully to Him with psalms
(Ps 95:2).

There is a connection between musical praise and the presence of God. When we worship in song, God's presence is manifest among us. Millions of Christians worldwide are discovering the power of God's presence in their lives as they worship the Lord privately and publicly.

Everywhere

C. S. Lewis said, "We may ignore, but we cannot evade the presence of God. The world is crowded with Him. He walks everywhere incognito."[1]

God is everywhere: He is omnipresent. He fills heaven and earth. He fills past, present, and future, all at the same time. One cannot ever leave or return to His presence. He is always everywhere.

Yet, the Bible tells us that after Adam and Eve had sinned:

They heard the sound of the Lord God walking in the garden in the cool of the day, and Adam and his wife hid themselves from the presence of the Lord God among the trees of the garden (Genesis 3:8).

In His Face

If God is absolutely everywhere, how can one hide from His presence? There must be another dimension of His presence. The Hebrew word for presence here means "at or to the face." It is a greater level of intimacy. When we get into someone's face, it is a place of vulnerability and connectedness.

When I come face-to-face with my wife, it is intimate and personal for both of us. So it is with God; He invites you to come face-to-face. Adam and Eve, the parents of the human race, experienced God up close and personal. They were often in God's face coversing and communing with Him.

Adam and Eve had always visited with God when He came to them. They probably to ran out to meet Him, but this day they had sinned and, therefore, held back. Their sin made them self-conscious and sin-conscious, and they did not want to get near God. Sin will take away your desire to get close to God.

As a result, Adam and Eve hid themselves behind the trees in the garden from the face, or intimacy, of God. But if this presence was God's omnipresence, He would be in and around the trees, and the couple wouldn't really be hidden from God's presence. This must mean there is another level of God's presence. It is what scholars call the *manifest* presence.

Touchable and Tangible

The manifest presence of God is an unusual aspect of Him that is revealed in a certain place and time. This dimension of God's presence is His revealed presence. It is the evident essence: His presence made visible and discernable. Though God is everywhere, He is not evident everywhere. The manifest presence is the touchable and tangible essence of God.

THOUGH GOD IS EVERYWHERE, HE IS NOT EVIDENT EVERYWHERE.

All Christians have access to this intimate presence of God, but some don't know how to find it. They think that perhaps it is God's choice whether He will reveal Himself to them. However, God has indicated in His Word how His revealed presence can be found.

Finding His Presence

Many believers assume that His presence is only evident when He decides to reveal Himself. However there is a wonderful secret God wants us to know—you can come into God's presence anytime and anywhere.

The awareness of Yahweh's splendor, essence, and power will be known throughout the earth. His glory is an aspect of His nearness revealed.

> For the earth will be filled
> With the knowledge of the glory of the Lord,
> As the waters cover the sea (Habakkuk 2:14).

The Scriptures encourage and command you to find the presence of God:

> Now set your heart and your soul to seek the
> Lord your God (1 Chronicles 22:19).

> Seek the Lord and His strength;
> Seek His face evermore! (Psalm 105:4).

Because the word presence is translated "at the face," the Psalmist is encouraging you to get up close and in the face of God. David, a passionate worshipper, had that desire:

> One thing have I asked of the Lord, that will I
> seek, inquire for, *and* [insistently] require: that
> I may dwell in the house of the Lord [in His
> presence] all the days of my life, to behold *and*
> gaze upon the beauty [the sweet attractive-
> ness and the delightful loveliness] of the Lord
> (Psalm 27:4 AMPCE).

It requires effort to find God's presence in your life and in your worship:

> You will seek Me, inquire for, *and* require
> Me [as a vital necessity] and find Me when

you search for Me with all your heart
Jeremiah 29:13 AMPCE).

You must be proactive to search for and seek God's presence. It is essential for a worshipper to have a passion for His presence.

> Whoever would come near to God must [necessarily] believe that God exists and that He is a rewarder of those who earnestly *and* diligently seek Him [out] (Hebrews 11:6 AMPCE).

When you persistently pursue the Lord's presence, you will find Him and know Him. As a God-seeker you will become a God-finder. However, there is a secret entrance to God's presence that few Christians are aware of. To find Him you must know where He is. The Bible invites us to enter into His presence, but how and where?

HOWEVER, THERE IS A SECRET ENTRANCE TO GOD'S PRESENCE THAT FEW CHRISTIANS ARE AWARE OF.

Entering His Presence

How do you come near to God? How do you enter His presence? Where is the entrance?

There are several portals to God's revealed presence. One of them is song. The Scripture says,

Come before His presence with singing
(Psalm 100:2).

The type of singing described here is loud, triumphant, and joyful. We can come into His presence, or face, with singing, but not any song. The key to entering God's presence is that this praise is not only musical but it is a spontaneous song.

This extemporaneous song is so personal that it comes right from our hearts like fresh bread—hot and right out of the oven of our hearts. This is our heavenly Father's favorite type of worship. We know this because He says He inhabits, or reveals Himself, in these spontaneous songs.

Yet You are holy,
O You who are enthroned upon the praises
[*tehillah*] of Israel (Psalm 22:3 NASB).

WHEN WE SING THIS PRAISE, GOD REVEALS THE POWER OF HIS PRESENCE.

The word *enthroned* in this scripture means, "to dwell or sit as judge." God sits as King and Judge in this praise and makes His presence and authority known. When we sing this praise, God reveals the power of His presence.

Enter into his gates with thanksgiving, and into his courts with praise [*tehillah*]: be thankful unto him, and bless his name. (Psalm 100:4).

This Scripture encourages you to go where God is and tells you how to do it. The entrance is giving thanks, or *towdah*. *Towdah* is the Hebrew word for a large group of believers who are worshipping vertically with extended hands. It is much like a congregation that gathers on the first day of the week to worship. They sing and lift their hands as a group.

Then Psalms 100:4 says to go further into the courts of His presence with praise. But this isn't any praise; this is *tehillah* praise, or vertical spontaneous singing. Psalms 40:3 says that when you sing to God spontaneously, you will find entrance into the King's courts, or presence.

It is such a wonderful experience to sing to God and know His revealed presence. It warms your heart and brings joy to your spirit. Do you realize that knowing how to enter God's presence gives you the freedom to enter God's revealed presence anytime and anywhere? Now it is up to you to get to know Him up close and personal.

Fish Out of Water

Because Adam and Eve were created to live in God's revealed presence, we know you were made for the presence of God as well. You are not complete without his manifest presence. If you live your life outside of His revealed presence, your life becomes very difficult. You quickly become like a fish out of water gasping for the breath— fighting for your life.

Like a fish that will die outside of the environment for which it was created, so you will die outside of the environment for which you were created. God's revealed presence is your health of body, soul, and spirit. All is at rest and all is secure in God's presence. There is safety from the things that torment and destroy. You are the happiest and most fulfilled in the intimate presence of God.

> You will show me the path of life;
> In Your presence *is* fullness of joy;
> At Your right hand *are* pleasures forevermore
> (Psalm 16:11).

In God's revealed presence there is abundant gladness and overflowing joy. Nothing satisfies your soul like the joy of being in God's revealed presence.

Study Guide

1. How would you describe the two dimensions of God's presence?
2. What is the difference between the two dimensions of God's presence?
3. What do you think it means to get in God's face?
4. How can you enter God's presence anytime you want to?
5. What would you say when someone asks you, "How can I find God's presence?"
6. Have you sung *tehillah* praise before? If so, what happened?

Scripture and Reflection

Read Psalm 27 and Psalm 100

1. After reading this chapter, how will you seek His presence?
2. How will a desire for His presence affect your life?
3. How will you enter God's revealed presence now?
4. From this moment on, what will you do in order to be in God's presence more throughout each day?
5. What things have hindered you from experiencing the manifest presence of God in your life?

Prayer

Heavenly Father, I desire Your presence in my life more than anything. Put in me a greater passion to seek You and then to find you. Cause my heart to want to know Your revealed presence. I want Your presence to be in my home, my relationships, my work, and my family. Holy Spirit, take me to greater depths of Your presence as I endeavor to live in the environment of Your revealed presence—worshipping You always. In Jesus' name, Amen.

13

Public

Worshipping churches seek to develop a worship
open to the supernatural, aware of mystery,
and committed to participation.
—*Robert Webber*

Josiah wondered if he woke up late, since the sun wasn't up yet. He jumped up from his floor mat and ran down the dirt path to Paul's house. It was time for the Lord's Day service.

All the believers in the village would gather in one of the leader's homes to worship. It had to be before dawn, because when the sun rose it symbolized when their Savior rose from the dead. The sun was about to break the horizon.

Paul began the prayers, Jewish style, and Josiah lifted up his voice to sing with the rest. They were chanting their *tehillah*, like some of the orthodox Jews did in the synagogue. Josiah liked the singing because he could be passionate. After all, his name meant *the fire of the Lord*. He could feel God's fire in his belly when he sang praise and prayers to Messiah.

There it was—the sun was rising, as was the faith in the hearts of the believers gathered in Paul's home. After he sang the reading of the Torah, Paul had the deacons serve the Agape Feast. They did this every time they met.

It was just a few months earlier when Josiah heard Paul share at a local synagogue that Messiah had come in the form of Jesus. That declaration startled Josiah and stirred his curiosity. After just a few days of contemplating what Paul had said, he decided to believe in Jesus as Messiah, and started meeting with Christians in their homes.

Taking the bread and wine in the Agape Feast became very special to Josiah. It embodied what Jesus had done for him. It was only about thirty years earlier that the Romans brutally killed Jesus and sealed Him in the cave. To everyone's surprise, when Mary came to the cave at dawn, it was open and vacant.

Paul finished the service with a hymn of David, and they stayed, talking about the exciting things that were happening among this young group of followers of Christ.

The Early Church

From the beginning of the early church, disciples of Jesus have gathered on the day of His resurrection to worship. The earliest gatherings of the disciples of Jesus were in homes, and as the attendance grew they met outdoors and in synagogues. Public worship was dynamic and powerful.

The first believers felt a mandate from God to gather to worship. This was the context in which each person had a part. Since the setting for gathering was in the home or synagogue, it was in the round and interactive. There was no sense of theater or performance of worship on behalf of the people. That developed later. Everyone participated, and some took turns leading a prayer or song.

THE FIRST BELIEVERS FELT A MANDATE FROM GOD TO GATHER TO WORSHIP.

Dr. Robert Weber stated, "The content of early Christian worship was Jesus Christ—his fulfillment of the Old Testament, His birth, life, death, resurrection, ascension, and coming again."[1]

The structure of early church worship gathering was the reading the Word of God, prayers, hymns, and benedictions. It was sealed with the Eucharist, also called the Lord's Supper.

A Habitation

> Now, therefore, you are no longer strangers
> and foreigners, but fellow citizens with the
> saints and members of the household of God,
> having been built on the foundation of the
> apostles and prophets, Jesus Christ Himself
> being the chief corner*stone,* in whom the
> whole building, being fitted together, grows
> into a holy temple in the Lord, in whom you
> also are being built together for a dwelling
> place of God in the Spirit (Ephesians 2:19–22).

There is an incredible mystery that occurs when the Body of Christ gathers together to lift up its exalted Head—Jesus.

God's people assemble with everyone providing part of a spiritual habitat for God.

The Gathering

All believers that gather together in a local church are being formed into a spiritual temple in which God wants to dwell. There is a divine mandate and blessing in the act of coming together as the Body of Christ in worship. The author of Hebrews encouraged the assembly:

> Not forsaking or neglecting to assemble together [as believers], as is the habit of some people, but admonishing (warning, urging, and encouraging) one another, and all the more faithfully as you see the day approaching (Hebrews 10:25 AMPCE).

WE CONGREGATE IN ORDER TO CELEBRATE, TO COMMUNICATE, TO COMMEMORATE, AND TO COMMUNE.

All those who have given their lives to Christ are to respond to the sacred call to congregate. There is a divine purpose in coming together as a family of believers. We congregate in order to celebrate, to communicate, to commemorate, and to commune. We celebrate in praise and worship, we communicate the story of God, we commemorate the Lord's Supper, and we commune with Him in His revealed presence. Believers of Christ gather together to worship, to edify each other, and to witness to the world.

The Sacrifices

Prior to Jesus changing how we are to worship, God's people gathered to offer material sacrifices, such as animals, birds, and grain. Today, however, we gather with other believers to offer spiritual sacrifices to God. We don't bring live animals to sacrifice in worship as God required under the old covenant. Under the new covenant of grace, we offer up spiritual sacrifices.

This is how the apostle Peter described us:

> You also, as living stones, are being built up a spiritual house, a holy priesthood, to offer up spiritual sacrifices acceptable to God through Jesus Christ (1 Peter 2:5).

The spiritual sacrifices God accepts from you through Jesus are the lifting of your hands, singing, praising, dancing, bowing, kneeling, prostrating, and praying. These sacrifices become spiritual when we engage our spirit and the Holy Spirit.

As mentioned before, it is your heart attitude that makes your external acts of worship spiritual. Just as the sacrifice of praise—the fruit of your lips—is spiritual when your heart is engaged, so is your singing, praying, dancing, and lifting of hands.

Paul instructed the early believers to offer their bodies in worship to God as a spiritual act:

> I appeal to you therefore, brethren, *and* beg of you in view of [all] the mercies of God, to make a decisive dedication of your bodies [presenting all your members and faculties] as a living sacrifice, holy (devoted, consecrated) and well pleasing to God, which is your reasonable (rational, intelligent) service *and* spiritual worship (Romans 12:1 AMP).

Jesus in the Middle

When believers gather in worship, a supernatural phenomenon occurs—Jesus joins the gathering. He said,

> For where two or three are gathered together
> in My name, I am there in the midst of them
> (Matthew 18:20).

Jesus joins believers who gather in His name—not for preaching only or horizontal singing, but for the purpose of worshipping the Father. Paul writes,

> We see Jesus ... saying,
>   "I will declare Your name to My brethren;
>   In the midst of the assembly I will sing
> praise to You" (Hebrews 2:9, 12).

When Jesus spiritually joins His believers in worship, He does not go to the platform, sing with the worship team, or sit with the pastors; rather, He joins the congregation—the family of believers. This reveals the heart of our great Shepherd. He does not want to disconnect but to be connected: not better than, but servant of all. He does not bring attention to Himself but blends with the worshippers. He mingles with us to become one with us. He is relational and interactive. Jesus is our example and the leader of worship.

Jesus values the act of engaging your spirit in song. When Jesus joins the worship of the church family (the "called out" ones), He sings. Our Savior sings as the leader of the choir of worshippers He redeemed.

WHEN JESUS JOINS THE WORSHIP OF THE CHURCH FAMILY (THE "CALLED OUT" ONES), HE SINGS.

It is important to note Jesus doesn't sing horizontal songs. Jesus sings to an audience of One. He sings praise to His Father. He doesn't sing *about* the Father, rather, He joins His brothers and sisters in singing *to* the Father. Jesus is an example of what to do when you worship. Worship as Jesus modeled it is full of spontaneous singing in vertical worship.

The Pastors

Though the leader in your public worship is Jesus, your human leaders have a role as well. It is important to understand the role of the leadership in worship. This understanding will help you engage and connect more spiritually in your worship.

Christian leaders are to be facilitators of worship. They are not to force, demand, or exercise their will on the Lord's flock. As shepherds, they follow the leading of the great Shepherd, listening to and obeying Him, and thereby leading the Lord's flock through encouragement and example, with pastoral care. Shepherds are to lead you to the still waters and green pastures of God's presence.

The pastors of the congregation are not only facilitators in connecting with God, they are also the chief worshippers. More than anyone else, they have a responsibility to be worshippers. Pastors are to live a life of worship and maintain the presence of God in their hearts and homes. As priests unto God, their first responsibility, as it is with you, is to minister to God. A priest is one who ministers to God and then to the people.

> Then the priests, the sons of Levi, shall come near, for the Lord your God has chosen them to minister to Him and to bless in the name of the Lord (Deuteronomy 21:5).

Just like Moses did, pastors spend time on the mountain of God's presence. When they speak as leaders, they speak not only with the heart of a shepherd but also with the witness of the power and presence of God. The presence of God empowers leaders to speak, sing, feed, and care for the flock of God with spiritual discernment; therefore, they must live in constant connection with the Holy Spirit and God's manifest presence.

Pastor Robert Morris once said to a large gathering of pastors, "If you are not worshipping, then your church probably is not a worshipping church." He challenged the pastors present to begin their prayer time with singing out loud and inviting God's presence, before making their prayer requests.

The Worship Leaders

Leaders of worship also have a key role in public worship. They are atmospheric engineers. Like greenhouse gardeners, they maintain the right climate in the garden of the gathering.

One of the key responsibilities of worship leaders is to create an atmosphere of hunger for God in corporate worship. They do that by preparing the atmosphere of their spirit and then creating a spiritual atmosphere of worship in the gathering. Worship leaders should focus on facilitating spiritual worship and the resulting encounter with Jesus.

There are five main responsibilities of a worship leader: be a worshipper; raise up worshipping musicians; create an atmosphere in the corporate gathering; facilitate believers' connecting with Jesus; and step out of the way for the Bride and the Bridegroom to commune.

The Worship-Leading Team

The team of musicians and singers facilitate the congregation's worship. The Biblical principle of worship leading comes from a song David sang.

Come before His presence with singing
(Psalm 100:2).

THE WORSHIP TEAM IS A "HELPS MINISTRY" THAT GIVES THE MELODY, RHYTHM, AND LYRICS FOR THE CONGREGATION TO SING.

The musicians and the singers are key to helping the church family come before God in song. The worship team is a "helps ministry" that gives the melody, rhythm, and lyrics for the congregation to sing. Using the tools of music, the team serves the congregation to connect spiritually with God through song. The worship team should not be the congregation's focus. Its purpose is to lead God's people to Jesus and then get out of the way.

Similarly, the Lord's focus is not on the worship team but on the congregation. The worship team should never desire to look good in the eyes of Jesus' Bride, but rather to be pleasing in the eyes of the Bridegroom. Their hearts and spirits should be prepared well for the spiritual act of facilitating worship. This can be done through personal worship, meditating on God's Word, fasting, and praying. Since worship is *in Spirit*, then you can prepare for worship by singing *in the Spirit* and praying *in the Spirit*. Doing those two things go a long way to prepare the worship team member to be a vessel whom God can use to bring His people into His revealed presence.

The Worshipper

It is the responsibility of all the worshippers to follow the leading of the Lord in worship and at the same time follow their spiritual leaders.

Paul taught the early church how to worship by saying,

> Whenever you come together, each of you
> has a psalm, has a teaching, has a tongue,
> has a revelation, has an interpretation
> (1 Corinthians 14:26a).

Everyone in the early church had something they wanted to contribute. Paul was telling them to prefer each other, to build up each other, and to wait for the right time by adding,

> Let all things be done for edification
> (1 Corinthians 14:26b).

Leaders are not the center of worship—the congregants are. The Lord joins in worship songs of the people. We should come to all public worship services ready to vibrantly worship despite what the worship team does or sings. Whether you like the songs or not, press past the music and connect with the Lord. Be consistent in your private and public worship by engaging with God spiritually.

The Eucharist

The Lord's Table can be a high point of worship. Jack Hayford wrote in his book *Explaining Worship,* "There is nothing more central to the worship life of the Church than that which Jesus founded by His death and resurrection—the feast of worship at the Lord's table."[2] At the Lord's Table, we not only celebrate Jesus' death and resurrection, but also we experience a reenactment of it. It is a dramatization of the work of salvation. The worshipper hears, sees, tastes, and smells the symbols of Christ's death in the bread and the wine.

Biblical worship is rooted in the Christ event—Jesus' death, burial, and resurrection—which is to be celebrated and remembered when we gather. When you worship, you celebrate what Christ did to redeem you and bring you into relationship with your heavenly Father.

This reenactment is also called the Eucharist, which means thanksgiving. The Eucharist should be a festive event and not a morbid one. It is about what Christ has done for you by dying on the cross and rising from the dead—freeing you from the power of death, hell, and sin. What a glorious victory! For those reasons you give Jesus joyful gratitude.

The New Song

There is a key principle that is connected with spiritual worship and the presence of God. As we saw earlier, it is what the Old Testament calls praise (*tehillah*) a new song (*hadas sir*), and the New Testament calls the *spiritual song*.

Speaking of God, the psalmist says,

> He has put a new song in my mouth—
> Praise to our God (Psalm 40:3)

This is a divinely imparted song. God puts a fresh, original song in your mouth. A new song is a personal song that is original with you. It is not a song already written that you have never heard before but a fresh song you sing.

The new song is sung mostly in private worship, but it can be sung in public worship as well. The worship leadership should allow spaces between songs or in the arrangement, or allot time for you to sing your own personal song to God.

The Bible often instructs us to sing new songs in vertical worship.

> Praise the Lord!
> Sing to the Lord a new song,
> *And* His praise in the assembly of saints
> (Psalm 149:1).
> Sing to Him a new song;
> Play skillfully with a shout of joy (Psalm 33:3).

This song is a spontaneous or extemporaneous song that you compose from your heart to the Lord. It is the difference between trying to express your love to your spouse by giving them a card with someone else's words or writing your own words. One is nice but the other is more personal.

USING YOUR OWN WORDS IN WORSHIP IS MUCH MORE PERSONAL THAN USING OTHER PEOPLE'S WORDS.

Most Christians find it impersonal to read another person's prayers when they pray to the Lord. Yet we read another person's lyrics when we sing to God. It is not as personal as using our own words. So you see, using your own words in worship is much more personal than using other people's words, just as using your own words when you pray is much more personal than using someone else's prayers.

What would you do if someone asked you to pray, but gave you a prayer to read? Would you say, "I want to pray in my own words"? Likewise, when given lyrics to sing, you could also say, "I want to sing in my own words." This is a deeper level of worship. Singing your own words to God is much more meaningful and personal than singing the words penned by a professional songwriter.

Public worship has many different elements, and all of them should be sincere, biblical in principle, and done for the correct purpose. That is why knowing what the Bible says about worship is absolutely critical for our services to please the Lord. Worship of the Lord's Bride is for the Bridegroom only. It takes discipline and discernment by leaders to keep the purpose and actions of the public worship service correctly focused.

Study Guide

1. What occurs when you assemble with other believers to worship?
2. Does Jesus join us in worship? If so, where?
3. What does Jesus do when we worship?
4. What is the role of the worship leader and the worship team in public worship?
5. What spiritual sacrifices should you offer to God?
6. How is the new song more personal and intimate than singing other people's songs?

Scripture and Reflection

Read 1 Peter 2:4–12 and Hebrews 10:19–25

1. Have you sung a new song in worship before? What does it mean to you?
2. How will you view the public worship service differently because of this session?
3. What personal barriers have hindered your expression in public worship?
4. How do you want the Eucharist to impact your worship?

Prayer

Heavenly Father, I commit to engage in true worship when I am in public worship with fellow believers. Give me the freedom to express myself to You. Increase my awareness of the presence of Jesus as He joins us to worship You. Crown our worship with Your presence as we gather in Your name and worship as one body—Your bride. In Jesus' name, Amen.

14

Verdict

Don't let life affect your worship;
let your worship affect your life.
—*LaMar Boschman*

The judge slammed the gavel down and declared, "Order!"
"But your honor, I do worship!" The defendant
protested.

"We examined the evidence, and there is no proof that
you are a worshipper!" the judge replied. "You stated your
case. What more do you have to add?"

The defendant had been arrested and charged for not
being a worshipper. It carried a mandatory sentence of an
unfulfilled life. He didn't like the jury's decision and protested the verdict.

"I go to church almost every weekend. I sing the songs
and listen to the messages."

"But do you worship other days and in other places as
well?" the judge asked. "Do you worship in all circumstances or any situation?"

"I try when I remember."

"Not good enough!" The judge replied. "You are just a
weekend worshipper!"

With that she slammed the gavel down again.

"This jury has found the defendant guilty of not being a worshipper. He is guilty as charged!"

With those words the defendant's heart sank. *No one told me how important worship is to God, and how it is for my own good.*

Why didn't my church teach me how to be a worshipper? I was there almost every weekend. Why didn't the worship leader or pastor ever explain what a worshipper is? It is not right, he mumbled to himself.

The Bible school I attended only taught worship music. They had classes on how to play the guitar for worship. I wasn't taught how to be a worshipper!

With determination he declared in his heart, *While serving my sentence, I will find out how to be a worshipper and become one! I want to please God and fill my life with his presence. I will no longer just sing along to the worship leader. I will worship with all my heart and soul. In the morning and throughout the day, God will hear my praise.*

As you have discovered, just because you go to a worship service and engage in the activity called worship does not mean you have worshipped. Likewise, because you attend worship service and participate in worship music does not mean you are a worshipper. So how do you know if you are?

Profile

We have come to the final chapter and to a final question. How do you know if you are a worshipper? If someone asks a teacher what he does for a living, he probably would reply, "I am a teacher." He says that because He spends most of his time teaching. Similarly, you know you are a worshipper when what you do the most is worship.

Worshippers don't just worship on weekends. They engage with God in worship every day and sometimes all day. Continual worship is central to the life of a worshipper, and should be for every Christian. A worshipper offers the sacrifice of praise to God continually.

> From the rising of the sun to its going down
> The Lord's name *is* to be praised (Psalm 113:3).

Endless eulogy, ceaseless celebration, and perpetual praise are the earmarks of a worshipper. Worshippers don't wait for perfect circumstances to worship, and they don't let current situations keep them from worshipping. They also exhibit worship throughout their daily lives, as they honor God with acts of service and evangelism.

Obligation

If you want to have a meaningful relationship with God, you must worship. We have no choice whether to worship because it is our responsibility. Paul said,

> We make it our aim ... to be well pleasing to
> Him (2 Corinthians 5:9).

I am sure it is your earnest desire to do what God expects of you and to please Him. You want to praise Him and please Him at all times—even in difficult situations.

There is a song in the Bible:

> Though the fig tree may not blossom,
> Nor fruit be on the vines;
> Though the labor of the olive may fail,
> And the fields yield no food;
> Though the flock may be cut off from the fold,
> And there be no herd in the stalls —
> Yet I will rejoice in the Lord,
> I will joy in the God of my salvation
>   (Habakkuk 3:17–18).

Though you have no money in your savings account and your checkbook is overdrawn; though the fridge and cupboard are empty and you were just laid off your job, yet you resolve to worship and rejoice in the Lord.

THE FIRST STEP IN BECOMING A WORSHIPPER IS TO WORSHIP IN SPITE OF YOUR CIRCUMSTANCES.

The first step in becoming a worshipper is to worship in spite of your circumstances. Fair-weather worshippers worship only when they feel good about life, or when things are going well. But real worshippers worship in and through all situations.

It is challenging to worship God when circumstances are hard and your feelings are out of sorts. It takes a mature worshipper to worship in difficult times.

The Bible tells of when King David had learned his child was sick. He laid it before the Lord in prayer. Nevertheless, the child passed away. Then David worshipped God in His pain:

> So David arose from the ground, washed and anointed himself, and changed his clothes; and he went into the house of the Lord and worshipped (2 Samuel 12:20).

Some people couldn't worship God after a death of a loved one. However, a worshipper does. He goes to the place that means the most to him—the presence of God.

Unreasonable

Would it be reasonable to say that God wants spiritual intensity in your worship? Surely He wants your worship to be your utmost for His highest. Our Father wants you to worship Him in four parts your being—with all your heart, soul, strength, and mind (see Luke 10:27).

Wholehearted worshippers are unreasonable in their lavish adoration. When you worship God wholeheartedly, you give Him everything. You are excessive and extravagant—extremely generous with your time, feelings, attitude, and energy.

WHOLEHEARTED WORSHIPPERS ARE UNREASONABLE IN THEIR LAVISH ADORATION.

Second, God wants you to love Him with all your soul. How do you do that? It involves your emotions.

> Bless (affectionately, gratefully praise) the
> Lord, O my soul; and all that is [deepest] within
> me, bless His holy name! (Psalm 103:1 AMP).

You are to worship God with deep passion and full emotion. God made you an emotional being. To express your emotions is natural. When your heart overflows within you but you subdue your emotions, you are acting unnaturally. Some of us have been told not to show our emotions in public worship; however, the Bible says the opposite. Just as you shouldn't hold back your emotional expressions to your spouse, so you should not hold them back in worship to God. Your worship should be extravagant, expressive, and emotional. The Lord delights in this kind of worship.

Third, you should love God with all your strength—your physical strength. In Chronicles we read:

> David and all Israel merrily celebrated before
> God with all their might, with songs and lyres
> and harps and tambourines and cymbals and
> trumpets (1 Chronicles 13:8 AMPC).

How did David and the people celebrate with all their strength? Can you imagine what that looked like? It most likely was physical and highly expressive. Did they jump, dance, shout, clap, scream, throw up their hands, or sing loudly to God? They probably did all that and so much more.

Fourth, the Lord wants you to love Him with your entire mind. This requires focusing your intellect and mental capacities on God. Contemplating who God is and what He has done, and then meditating on Him, is loving Him with your mind. It may require commemoration, consideration, and contemplation.

When you adore God by thinking on His character and attributes, it impacts your spirit. Upon observation and examination of what and who He is, you will be inspired, and, sometimes, overwhelmed. Adoring God with your mind involves contemplating and meditating on His greatness and holiness—all of His pristine perfections.

Another aspect of loving God with all your mind is to concentrate on God in worship. Whole-minded worshippers are not easily distracted. They are focused and totally God-conscious in public and private worship.

Notice the order of the words in Luke 10:27—heart, soul, strength, and mind. Luke listed them in order of importance. The most important is first. You must have heart attitude. The second and third words are the ways you express that attitude. The last is mind—the least expressive, but still an important part of your worship of God; using your intellect to contemplate God.

Contagious

Worshippers are also infectious. They are abandoned to God, expressive, and overflowing with love and affection for

Him. When people see this kind of abandonment, they usually want it for themselves! Worshippers rub off on others, creating a hunger for God and a desire to be connected with Him, just as they are.

WORSHIPPERS COLOR OUTSIDE THE LINES AND SING OUTSIDE THE ARRANGEMENT.

Worshippers don't need a bulletin, or a call to worship, or a worship leader to encourage them to go vertical. They don't need to be told to sing out or to lift their hands. Worshippers color outside the lines and sing outside the arrangement. They can worship in any place and at any time.

Priest

You are called by God to be a king and priest to Him. He has:

Made us kings and priests to our God. (Revelation 5:10).

As a priest, you come before His presence and worship Him, on behalf of yourself and others. As a king, you rule with His authority.

To Him who loved us and washed us from our sins in His own blood, and has made us kings and priests to His God and Father ... (Revelation 1:5–6).

Kings and priests don't serve only on weekends. They are fully committed and fully vested to be full-time rulers and full-time worshippers.

Broken

There is nothing that distinguishes a worshipper from a non-worshipper more than a broken spirit. Since you worship from your spirit, it should not be defiled with ego, evil, sin, and darkness. Worshippers spend time in God's presence and allow the Master to tame their wild and uncontrolled spirits.

The Bible says that the pure in heart will see God (Matt 5:8). You become pure in your heart by submitting your heart to the Lord. Like a wild horse, you must have your unruly spirit broken and your rebellious heart tamed. This will bring purity and honesty to your worship.

> The sacrifice you desire is a broken spirit.
> You will not reject a broken and repentant
> heart, O God (Psalm 51:17 NLT).

Study Guide

1. How would you describe a worshipper to someone?
2. Which characteristics of a worshipper do you find most unique?
3. Would God describe you as a worshipper? Why or why not?
4. What person in your life would you say is a worshipper? Why?
5. What has impacted you the most as you have studied the mystery of worship?
6. What are the priorities of a worshipper?

Scripture and Reflection

Read Psalm 103, Psalm 113, Matthew 22:36–40
1. What does loving God with all your heart, soul, mind, and strength mean to you?
2. What have been your biggest struggles in worshipping God with all your heart, soul, mind, and strength?
3. What will you do differently to develop a reputation as a worshipper of God?
4. How will your life as a worshipper be different as a result of this study?

5. Describe your new life as a complete worshipper of God?

Prayer

Heavenly Father, I want so much to be an expressive and extravagant worshipper. I want to give You my best and most honest worship. Equip me to be a worshipper that pleases You. Help me be an example of a worshipper to everyone in my life. Holy Spirit, move in my heart to groom me to be the worshipper the Father is looking for. I give my life, my heart, and affections to You. In Jesus' name, Amen.

Suggestions for Group Facilitators

This book will inspire discussion and interaction when read and commented on as a group. It is an excellent resource for worship teams, choirs, Bible Colleges, book studies, or life groups. Instead of lecturing, I suggest that you facilitate discussion by encouraging each participant to share their thoughts and responses to what they are reading or discussing. Remember that the Holy Spirit will not only speak through you but also through those present.

1. Encourage participants to bring their Bibles and this book to each session.
2. Begin each session with sincere and worshipful prayer. Invite the Holy Spirit to bring revelation and inspiration to each one present.
3. Review what is covered in previous sessions and ask what impressions they have. This will facilitate discussion.
4. Encourage participants to respond with comments and questions as you review Scripture and discussion questions.
5. Use aids in your discussion, such as a white board or

paper easel. List major points or questions you want to discuss with the group.

6. You can draw out thoughts and experiences from the group by asking them to share out of their own personal experience. You can ask, "Have you experienced this? How did you feel about it at the time?"

7. Your goal as a facilitator is to help each participant apply the principle being discussed to his or her life. The questions are designed to do this.

About the Author

For four decades, LaMar Boschman has helped people connect with the presence of God in spiritual worship and music of the kingdom. He is one of the pioneers and fathers of contemporary worship. As a prolific author, worship leader, and keynote speaker, LaMar Boschman has impacted churches and leaders around the world. His gifts have changed church cultures and redefined the paths of many church leaders.

A sought-after speaker and mentor, LaMar Boschman is known for equipping others in transcendent worship. Here is a snapshot of LaMar in his own words:

> When I received my first guitar when I was fourteen, I remember the joy of writing and singing songs. At sixteen I recorded my first album with a couple of friends, and we sang wherever we were invited touring around western Canada. In Vancouver, I became part of a musically progressive church and discovered more praise and worship; my life would never be the same. I have led worship and taught about worship around the world. Today I teach seminars, speak at conferences, blog, write books, and mentor leaders.

Looking back to a time when we only worshipped with pianos, organs, and hymnbooks, there were a few of us who created the term "worship leader" and "worship team" at the first worship events in the U.S.

LaMar and his wife live in Dallas/Ft. Worth, Texas, and are members of Gateway Church where they both serve.

Connect with LaMar at LaMarBoschman.com

- Gain fresh revelation on spiritual principles that will empower your music, your worship life, and ministry by subscribing to LaMar's Blog
- Discover books, videos, and other resources from prominent leaders
- Schedule LaMar to speak at your event

Follow LaMarBoschman on Instagram, Twitter, Facebook, and YouTube.

Notes

1. Wired

1. Jack Hayford, *Explaining Worship* (Trent, UK: Sovereign World, 1996), 8.

2. Harold Best, *Unceasing Worship* (Downers Grove, IL: Intervarsity Press, 2003), 18.

2. Morphed

1. Jack Hayford, *Explaining Worship* (Trent, UK: Sovereign World, 1996), 7.

3. First

1. Judson Cornwall, *Things We Adore* (Shippensburg, PA: Destiny Image, 1991), 18.

4. Wonder

1. A. W. Tozer, *The Knowledge of the Holy* (New York: HarperSanFrancisco, 1961), 1.

5. Called

1. A. W. Tozer, *Worship: The Missing Jewel Of The Evangelical Church* (Camp Hill, PA: Christian Publications, 1992), 12.

2. Warren Wiersbe, *Real Worship* (Nashville, TN: Nelson, 1986), 17.

3. Matthew Henry's Commentary on the Whole Bible: New Modern Edition, Electronic Database Copyright © 1991 by Hendrickson Publishers, Inc.

6. Devotion

1. Donna-Marie Cooper O'Boyle, excerpt from *Mother Teresa and Me: Ten Years of Friendship* (Huntington, IN: Our Sunday Visitor, 2011), .https://aleteia.org/2016/09/02/6-inspiring-stories-from-people-who-met-mother-teresa/.

2. W.E. Vines, *Vine's Expository Dictionary of New Testament Words*. https://www.blueletterbible.org/search/Dictionary/viewTopic.cfm?topic=VT0003400.

3. http://biblehub.com/greek/4352.htm

4. Judson Cornwall, *Let Us Worship* (Bridge Publishing, South Plainfield, NJ, 1983), 66.

5. http://www.tentmaker.org/biographies/barclayquotes.htm.

6. Darlene Zschech, *Extravagant Worship* (Check Music Ministries, Castle Hill, NSW 1765 Australia, 2001), 11.

7. CeCe Winans, *Throne Room: Ushered Into the Presence of God* (Mobile, AL: Integrity Publishers, 2004), 49.

8. John Piper, *Desiring God: Meditations of a Christian Hedonist*, revised and expanded ed. (Colorado Springs, 2011), 79.

7. Mobile

1. Judson Cornwall, *Let Us Praise/Let Us Worship* (Bridge Logos, Alachua, FL 2006), 39.

8. Expressions

1. Bob Kauflin, *Worship Matters* (Wheaton, IL: Crossway Books, 2008), 170.

9. God Talk

1. John Piper, *What is Worship?* http://www.desiringgod.org/interviews/what-is-worship, accessed April 29, 2016.

2. International Standard Bible Encyclopedia, http://www.blueletterbible.org/search/Dictionary/viewTopic.cfm?topic=ET0003838,ITO009247,NT0005174,ST0000214.

11. Celestial

1. Leon Morris, *The Revelation of St. John* (Grand Rapids, MI: Wm. B. Eerdmans, 1969), 100.

12. Revealed

1. C.S. Lewis, *Letters to Malcolm: Chiefly on Prayer* (San Diego: Harvest, 1964), 75.

13. Public

1. Robert Webber, *Worship Old and New* (Grand Rapids, MI: Zondervan, 1982), 56.

2. Jack Hayford, *Explaining Worship* (Kent, England: Sovereign World, 1996), 24.